Rainbow Parenting

Rainbow Parenting

Your Guide
to Raising Queer Kids
and Their Allies

LINDZ AMER

ST. MARTIN'S
GRIFFIN
NEW YORK

First published in the United States by St. Martin's Griffin,
an imprint of St. Martin's Publishing Group

www.stmartins.com

Designed by Omar Chapa

Library of Congress Cataloging-in-Publication Data

Names: Amer, Lindz, author.
Title: Rainbow parenting : your guide to raising queer kids and their
    allies / Lindz Amer.
Description: First edition. | New York : St. Martin's Griffin, 2023. |
    Includes bibliographical references and index.
Identifiers: LCCN 2022058225 | ISBN 9781250836489 (trade paperback) |
    ISBN 9781250836496 (ebook)
Subjects: LCSH: Gender-nonconforming people. | Gender
    nonconformity. | Parenting.
Classification: LCC HQ18.55 .A447 2023 | DDC 649/.13—
    dc23/eng/20230110
LC record available at https://lccn.loc.gov/2022058225

Our books may be purchased in bulk for promotional, educational, or business use. Please contact your local bookseller or the Macmillan Corporate and Premium Sales Department at 1-800-221-7945, extension 5442, or by email at MacmillanSpecialMarkets@macmillan.com.

First Edition: 2023

10 9 8 7 6 5 4 3 2

For every queer and trans kid, I hope this helps

CONTENTS

SPREAD QUEER JOY

A Mission Statement

You know that saying, "If you give a [person] a fish, you feed [them] for a day. If you teach a [person] to fish, you feed [them] for a lifetime." The gender binary of the original proverb aside, in this book, we're going to learn how to fish together. No matter whether you're a parent, an educator, a librarian, a creator, or someone who picked this book off the shelf and flipped to the first page because the title sounded cool. Maybe you're queer or trans or nonbinary, but you were raised in the same cisheteronormative hellscape as the rest of us and don't know how to go about queer and gender-affirming parenting. Maybe your favorite cousin is nonbinary, and you want your kids to understand their identity but don't know how to start the conversation. Or maybe you're an educator who wants support in bringing queer and gender-affirming lessons into your classroom. Regardless of your individual context for coming to this book, you are here because you care about the littlest folks among us and are interested in creating a queer and gender-affirming environment around them where they can *thrive*. I call that *spreading queer joy*.

But what does that mean exactly? Do you have to run around in a unicorn onesie singing about Pride and rainbows? I mean, that's what I do every Wednesday afternoon, but it's definitely not a requirement. Spreading queer joy, for me, is a mission, a philosophy, a methodology, a pedagogy, a mode of being, a North Star, a thesis statement, a mantra. To *spread* is to act; it is something that can be done, it is active and motivated and driven and progressing forward with relentless momentum and exponential in its expansion. It is *queer*; different, unique, other, divergent, diverse, and stunningly beautiful. This queerness is intersectional, it is ubiquitous, and by that I mean that queerness is everywhere, it knows no bounds. Queerness exists across race, ethnicity, culture, geography, even species. Queer for me and my life has been the center; the rule, not the exception. And *joy* is unbridled happiness, kindness, rainbows, unicorns, glitter, and the best of our collective wildest imaginations. So much is held in these three words: spread queer joy. They are the blanket that comforts, the shield that protects, the glitter that glimmers, and the balm that heals.

I will guide you—yes *you,* dear reader—in spreading queer joy to everyone from your newborn to your great-great grandparents. This work is familial and ancestral, it is the work that will bring about the world that ought to be. Spreading queer joy is the work of utopia building, and to succeed we must all be builders, or to continue the metaphor, fisherfolk! If you teach someone to spread queer joy, they'll keep spreading it farther.

INTRODUCTION

HOW TO USE THIS BOOK

Hello! Welcome to my book! This book is for parents, educators, librarians, caretakers, siblings, niblings, aunts, uncles, cousins, grandparents, great-grandparents, etc., etc., etc. It's for anyone who is around prepubescent young people and wants to help raise them in a queer and gender-affirming space but might need a little help along the way. I'm here to help! I'm a *professional queer* who makes LGBTQ+ and social justice media for kids and families, breaking down these seemingly complex topics so literally anyone—even a three-year-old!—can understand them.

I've been doing this for the better part of a decade, starting with my work as an undergraduate studying and making queer theater for kids. I created my web series, *Queer Kid Stuff,* in 2016 and have been making queer-centered work for all ages on my own ever since. I've toured libraries, schools, and community centers all over the United States (in person and virtually). I write, produce, and perform my own work. I consult with fancy Hollywood folks on how they can make their stuff for kids more queer and trans-inclusive. I give keynotes and workshops and speak publicly about these issues with grown-ups—maybe you've seen my viral TED Talk? I've also worked at preschools, hosted many a one-year-old's birthday party, and been around early childhood music education pretty much my entire life. But I don't know everything, of course. The learning of this work is an ongoing lifelong journey that I'm still very much on. This book is a collection of the knowledge I have gained so far along my path and aims to help you learn how to spread queer joy.

Caveat: I am a queer and transmasc, nonbinary, white, able-bodied, neurodivergent,[1] Jewish person and can only speak to my own individual experiences. In researching this book, I consulted some truly brilliant experts who also make radical queer work for kids and come from different perspectives. They shared their thoughts, opinions, and experiences, but these pages don't contain all of the thoughts, opinions, and experiences of the LGBTQ+ community. Neither I nor the folks whose words I've included are a monolith, and while I've done everything in my power to be as comprehensive as possible, I've probably missed a few things. I encourage you to look at this book as a general overview so you can use the information within it as a springboard for your own deep dives into these topics. You'll find that this book introduces whole fields and wealths of information beyond what I can encapsulate here. Think about this text as the beginning of a lifelong journey full of infinite conversations between you and the young folks in your lives. The mission

---

1 Someone who is neurodivergent might have ADHD, be autistic, dyslexic, or have features we wouldn't consider "neurotypical." I'm still figuring out my particular diagnosis, but I'm still figuring out my particular diagnosis, likely some combination of ADHD and autism.

of this book is not a one-and-done. It's a philosophy for how to move forward as a grown-up with a responsibility to the young people around you to leave the world a little bit better than when you came into it.

You'll learn how to spread queer joy through what I call "rainbow parenting," using queer and gender-affirming parenting practices. But, what is that exactly, and why is it important? The short answer to the "what" of it all is that queer and gender-affirming parenting looks at parenting strategies through a queer and trans lens. We're approaching child-rearing and educating from a vantage point that does not assume that a child will ultimately identify as straight and cisgender. We're not assuming they will be queer or trans, either, but we are introducing them to the world with the idea that they can grow up to identify any which way, *including* queer and trans identities. For the long answer, you'll just have to keep reading!

We'll start by identifying the *big problem* we face: that queer people and kids exist in a world that does not center—or really even acknowledge—their experience. We'll work through some of the obstacles stopping us from fixing that problem, and look toward a potential solution within early childhood education, media, and parenting strategies. We'll unpack some of our own misconceptions around queerness and kids, and we'll begin to lay out a larger solution for how to solve this problem of ours by finding age-relevant, simple ways of talking about these topics with the young people in our lives.

I'll share bits and pieces of my own journey along the way as I developed my work bringing LGBTQ+ and social justice edutainment to preschoolers. Together, we'll learn how children develop their identities and why this work must start in infancy. We'll learn about our own unconscious biases and how to reshape our worldview to center perspectives that are not solely straight, white, cisgender, able-bodied, male, and Christian. We'll learn how to describe a world that *specifically* decenters straightness, whiteness, cisgenderedness, and maleness for kids. I'll share how I came to spreading queer joy, why I think it's important, how you can understand it for yourself, and how you can even teach others.

The bulk of the book is made up of age-based resource chapters focused on how we can approach LGBTQ+ and social justice topics throughout the early stages of young people's lives. We'll walk through four different stages of early childhood—infancy, toddlerhood, pre-K, and elementary school—and learn how to talk to kids about queerness, gender, sexuality, sex and health education, intersectionality, activism, and LGBTQ+ history.

These are the core concepts we have to understand in order to raise and support a generation of kids in a queer and gender-affirming way. They are our foundational pillars, upon which we can build to a more just future. Together, we'll work through ideas and concepts that will help you center queerness for yourself, start introducing these ideas to young people, and develop specific practices to create a queer and gender-affirming space.

Each chapter leads you through these age-relevant concepts and gives practical ways to engage young folks in these topics through suggested activities, conversation starters, book recommendations, and some key takeaways for you to think about as you're reading. That said, all of the language I use in this book demonstrates how I talk to grown-ups *and kids* about these topics. I'm breaking these ideas down for kids, but I'm also breaking them down for you. It's honestly more important that *you* understand these concepts first and foremost. When you have a firm grasp on these topics, that will give you the confidence to have conversations with kids and level up your knowledge on your own beyond what's covered in this book.

We'll start at the *very* beginning: infancy. I know it might seem silly to start *so early*; babies can barely say "baba" let alone tell you their pronouns. But I encourage you to think of infancy as a practice round! You can create a queer and gender-affirming environment in their nursery, babble to them about consent while you're changing their diaper, and start up your well-rounded book collection. We'll get these introductory conversations going in infancy as a solid road map for work we can do in the years ahead.

Then comes *toddlerhood*. Toddlers soak up every little thing around them as they explore their surroundings. Most toddlers won't have the cognitive ability to self-identify as anything but a tiny flailing human working on their fine and gross motor skills. But you can introduce them to big abstract concepts like queerness and difference, and develop healthy skills like body kindness and consent. Starting with *queerness* gets us all on the same page. It reorients and points us in the direction we need to take to follow the path of this work. Then there's age-relevant sex and health education. Maybe infancy and toddlerhood seem a little early to introduce ideas around consent and body kindness, but it will help you build a strong and confident foundation with the young people in your life and lay the groundwork for later conversations around our bodies.

Then we'll head to school for pre-K, where we'll dive headfirst into a basic understanding of gender, sexuality, even intersectionality and activism. As we move from toddlerhood into pre-K years, the kids in our lives are internalizing the world around them and developing their own identities. We can help them in that process by giving them specific tools and explorations around gender. We'll dismantle the ways in which our binary-gendered world functions and how we can put it back together for young folks while we practice vulnerable, honest, and transparent communication with them. This is a big step, because it's where we're building up the practical techniques and tools that will help us along the way.

Then we'll explore conversations around sexuality. As preschoolers build little lives of their own with their friends at school and in their community, they see examples of lots of different kinds of families, and their world becomes a bit more complicated. Talking about sexuality and what different families look like can help them process that world and flex their empathy muscles.

Then we'll make our way to kindergarten, building on our foundational understanding of gender to fully grasp trans and nonbinary identities, the full LGBT alphabet, and dig into intersectionality and everything that makes us who we are as whole humans. We'll get more practical about how you can help the young folks in your lives become change-makers themselves and supplement their education with LGBTQ+ history that isn't always taught in school.

It might seem like a lot for your kiddos to handle, but I urge you not to underestimate the tiny ones. They may be small, but they be mighty! Through these age-relevant conversations, we can reprogram our understanding of the world around us in order to scaffold that queer and gender-affirming environment we can gift to young people. This is where you have to dig deep to build the muscles necessary to carry out our mission.

This book is ordered in a way that the ideas build organically and cumulatively upon each other. The learning in this book isn't linear; think about it more like a spiral. We'll introduce topics, dig into them, then step into something else before circling back to the same topic and dig even deeper on the next pass. Because of this Slinky-like structure, I urge you not to skip around on your first read. If you come to this book with a four-year-old, you should still read the infancy chapter. You might not use the same techniques with your four-year-old, but you need to understand the basic principles laid out from the very beginning in order to give yourself enough context to start having age-relevant conversations with your preschooler. Take the full road map in on your first pass of this book, then feel free to roam around and come back to specific sections once you have a full understanding of the landscape.

With that in mind, these age-defined sections come with a *big* caveat that every single child is different. You know your child best, and you know what is most developmentally relevant to them. If your toddler is already asking questions that this book answers for kindergarteners, then listen to your child's needs over the structure of this book. Maybe your child is already in pre-K, but you're starting from scratch because you haven't known how to talk about these ideas before now. Or maybe you have a two-year-old *and* a five-year-old at completely different levels of understanding. Absorb what you can from these sections, keep what works, and throw out what doesn't. And hey, maybe you'll come up with techniques and ideas that are completely unique to you and your kids—that's awesome! What has worked for me might not work for you, and that's more than okay. Take this book as guide, not gospel.

I hope you can use this book as a starting point on your journey. With the help of a small team on a shoe-string budget, I've been able to reach a couple million people across the globe through my videos, podcasts, talks, and live performances, but I'm only one person. You can help spread queer joy exponentially by passing along the knowledge in these pages to every young person you know *and* the fellow grown-ups in your circle. You'll have your own unique journeys with your young folks, and that is more than okay. So let's get to it!

VENTURING UNDER THE DOORKNOB

Before we dig into the *why* and the *what,* let's discuss the *how,* which can be the most overwhelming part for folks approaching these topics with the kids in their lives. *How do I make these complicated topics simple enough for even a toddler to understand?* I know it seems daunting, but I promise there's a way. The not-so-secret secret is that it's a *lot* less complicated than you might think!

Here's where I divulge the secret of my trade. Back in undergrad, I took a class on playwriting in theater for young audiences taught by accomplished queer playwright Philip Dawkins. On our first day, he gave everyone a handout detailing a few best practices for writing plays for kids. The piece of advice he provided has stuck with me over the years as I've pursued this work: *write from under the doorknob.*

I found this visual metaphor incredibly powerful. It asks the writer to understand a child viewer's context by kneeling down to their level and looking up at the world as they do. From three feet off the ground, the world looks different: Everything is bigger; some things don't have names yet; some things are out of reach, while some are closer and more accessible. When grown-ups look at the world through a child's eyes, from "under the doorknob," we can understand the context through which they approach the world: with curiosity.

Talking to kids from under the doorknob is all about meeting them at their level. I'm not "dumbing" anything down; I'm simplifying it into a vocabulary they can relate to. I take concepts that are comprehensible to young children like fairness, love, family, and justice, and package those ideas in a familiar visual vocabulary through toys, animation, blocks, stuffed animals, picture books, and other mediums that are developmentally relevant. We can talk about big ideas by breaking them down small enough to fit into their universal truths. I'll walk you through some of the explanations and conversations that have worked for me, but this is where you can get creative on your own with language and visual vocabulary that comes from your household and cultural background that the kids around you are familiar with.

We have a responsibility as grown-ups to guide them in their early years toward an understanding of our world that will best allow them to live their lives with authenticity in pursuit of happiness. I believe that in order to do that for every child, not only the seemingly normative ones, we have to impart a queer-centric, anti-racist vision of the world we strive toward while acknowledging the realities we are working to change. We have to reframe our own understanding of the world in order to teach children toward achieving a better future. Through understanding this responsibility, I've constructed a lens through which we can approach these ideas in a way that is understandable to young children—and, honestly, pretty much everyone—from under the doorknob.

MAKING MISTAKES AND STAYING VULNERABLE

I've made many mistakes over the years in doing this work, but the biggest was during the first season of *Queer Kid Stuff*. I wrote and shot a series of episodes breaking down the letters in LGBT.[2] The first video explained the acronym as an umbrella term for the LGBTQ+ community, and I went over multiple iterations of the acronym and what the letters stand for. The following videos in the series broke down each letter: "L for Lesbian," "G for Gay," "B for Bisexual," and "T for Trans!" I also included videos on "I for Intersex" and "A for Asexual."

But my mistake came in the video "B Is for Bisexual." I thought I knew what I was talking about but, really, I didn't. This was a result of the hubris of someone in their early twenties who found a modicum of internet success that they weren't quite ready for in the first project they did out of grad school, but that's no excuse. I didn't do my research, and that was irresponsible. The video defined bisexuality as an identity in which a person can love and be attracted to both boys and girls. This definition is outdated. It's based in a binary understanding of gender identity—something I attempted to dismantle within the series but wasn't fully knowledgeable in yet—and erases trans and nonbinary people within a bisexual identity. Ironically, identities I now hold myself as a nonbinary bisexual person!

The updated definition of bisexual is an identity where a person can love and be attracted to people of the same

---

2 Some terms and ideas might come up throughout this story that you're not familiar with yet. Don't worry, we'll get there later in the book! I tell this story to talk about my own faults and how I've worked through them. No need to get hung up on the details yet!

and different genders or multiple genders. The term is inclusive of trans and nonbinary people who identify as bisexual themselves, and doesn't confine bisexual attraction to the gender binary. When viewers called me out for the original video on social media, I got defensive and doubled down. It was difficult for me to distinguish between valid criticism from my community and just plain trolling from the hateful dissenters who wanted me to drink bleach. You'd think it would be easier to differentiate, but when you're in the middle of a barrage of harassment, it's hard to see the forest for the trees. Again, not an excuse for the harm I caused.

As I settled more firmly into my activism, I started to take my position as someone with an audience a lot more seriously. I worked privately with my then-therapist on my defensive reflex (something I'm still working on), and slowly learned more about my mistake and why it was harmful. I learned that I couldn't know everything, and figured out that I could, and should, reach out to others with more expertise when I wanted to represent an identity or experience that was not my own. I started bringing more guests onto the show, and finding resources and groups that could help me learn and grow into this component of what I do. I never sought out activism, but accepting that label as an essential facet of what I wanted to do was a necessary step toward making my work as good and as impactful as it could possibly be. If I wanted to do the most net good, I had to make sure my work met expectations. Meeting this bar was especially important because there is (still) very little queer-centered work for kids and families. With so few resources, the audience I serve needs the work to be good. There is very little room for mediocrity.

As I grew as an activist, it became more and more

apparent how egregious my mistake had been in that initial video on bisexuality and my unwillingness to understand my mistake in the moment. I added a "do-over" video to our very long slate of future episode topics—a list that still sits on my phone unfinished to this day. Between all of the videos on our slate, we were able to get to the new bisexuality video in our fourth season. I wanted to do it right this time so I asked for help. I asked fellow activist YouTuber Taylor Behnke, a Black bisexual activist, organizer, and creator to collaborate on the episode and to help me write the script and guest host. But what was most important to me was making sure I owned up to the mistakes I made in the first video and acknowledge the harm I caused. I want to make sure that my young viewers know that I am human. That I make mistakes. That even though I am a grown-up, I am not perfect; and that when we make mistakes, it is important for us to take responsibility for them, apologize gracefully, learn from that mistake, make every effort to correct it, and move forward with a resolve to do better next time.

I take a lot of inspiration from Fred Rogers, and this is something he was spectacular at. He kept mistakes and mess-ups in the final cuts of episodes of *Mister Rogers' Neighborhood* in an industry (film and television) that likes to be squeaky-clean at the final cut. I'm telling you the story of my own fumble to encourage you to be brave when you approach these conversations and topics with the young ones in your lives. Even though you are a grown-up and kids look up to you, you are still human. You are allowed to make mistakes. You are allowed to be messy. You are allowed to not know everything. Take the pressure off yourself to be perfect in this work; there is no such thing. All we can do is try to do the best that we can, make sure we are transparent in our communication, and take responsibility for our actions when we mess up. All we can do is try to do as little harm as possible.

But remember to be kind to yourself. We're covering a *lot* of ground here! We're going to talk about gender identity and expression, drag and clothes and toys, the difference between being cis versus trans, toxic masculinity and transmisogyny,[3] nonbinary gender identity *and* the gender spectrum. That's a LOT of gender stuff!

But I want to reassure you that while this is potentially an overhaul of your entire conception of gender, sexuality, etc., you don't need to impart everything in here to the kids in your life all at once, and you are not expected to be an expert right off the bat. This process takes time. You can work on this with the young folks in your life at a pace that makes sense for you. And you can practice your own vulnerability by admitting to yourself and to them that you do not know everything. You are also learning about these things and working on yourself every day. You are on this journey *with them*.

Go into this learning with courage, an open mind, and a commitment to moving forward with the understanding that you will probably stumble along the way. You don't need to be afraid of not knowing something. The beauty that lies within this journey with a young person is that you can go through it together. This is *especially* important to model with young

---

3 The term "transmisogyny," originally coined by Julia Serano, describes the intersections of transphobia and misogyny that trans women and transfeminine people experience. You can also blend the terms "transmisogyny" and "misogynoir"—originally coined by Black feminist Moya Bailey—to talk about "transmisogynoir," describing the intersections of race and gender that Black trans women uniquely experience.

kids. You are not all knowing! You are not omniscient! You are a human being and you don't know everything. If you don't know something, be honest about that and figure out a way to fill that gap in your knowledge. When you come across a word you don't know, pause and make a plan to learn *together*. The internet can be a beautiful thing—use it. These moments are fantastic opportunities to learn something *with* the young person (or people) in your life.

I spent way too much time stewing in my own self-doubt and being scared of everything I didn't know, without realizing that the knowledge I was looking for could only be found through collaboration. I had to learn to actively practice vulnerability—a lesson you can take into your work with the young people in your lives as you move through this book. As Brené Brown, one of the foremost researchers on vulnerability, shame, and leadership, so wisely reminds us, "Vulnerability is the birthplace of innovation, creativity, and *change* [my emphasis]."

HOW I GOT HERE
Content Warning: misgendering and childhood gender trauma

Vulnerability doesn't come naturally or easily for me. For a person who has spent years performing in theaters and on camera to thousands, even millions, of people, I consider myself a rather private person—but I'm getting over this mild personal discomfort because I think my journey is particularly important for you to understand. Right now, I identify as a queer and transmasc nonbinary person who uses they and them pronouns. Basically that means that I identify as neither a man nor a woman. I'm somewhere in the middle—simultaneously neither and both—and my gender expression is generally on the masculine side of things.

What you also need to know is that I have built my career on this particular knack I have for being able to explain the nuances of gender, sexuality, identity, and activism so pretty much anyone can understand them—including preschoolers—but I wasn't always this way. I didn't pop out of the womb with a completely different understanding of the world. I grew up in a straight, white, cis-centered home. I hope my story will show you how I've come to be where I am today, and how you can join me in doing this important anti-racist, queer, and trans-centered work sooner than you think and even inspire others to join in. The more the merrier!

I'll start with a story. When I was eight, my camp counselor mistook me for a boy.

It was Jewish day camp in Westchester, New York, and it was our first week with a new set of counselors. We were walking from the arts-and-crafts pavilion to the pool for swimming lessons before lunch. The boys took the path to the left down to their changing rooms, and the girls took the path to the right. I followed the girls to the right when I heard a voice calling to me:

"Where are you going? Come with us." The new male counselor waved me over.

I hesitated. In the weeks before, I had always walked with the girls to the right, but he was the counselor. He was in charge. He knew what was right, theoretically. So I turned and followed the boys. We got to the boys changing room and something between confusion and panic set in. I was surrounded by little boys and their little penises. Penises everywhere! I'd never seen a penis before—I grew up with three sisters. I pulled out my one-piece tie-dye swimsuit from my backpack next to my smooshed turkey sandwich. I knew I'd be found out soon. I took a deep breath, stripped down, and slipped on my swimsuit as fast as my little hands could manage while covering my body. But it was too late. My body was different from the rest. I stood up straight and turned toward my counselor, ready for the pool. His jaw dropped and his eyes widened. He grabbed my bag from the bench and gripped my arm. There was no time to slip on my flip-flops. He ran with me back up the path and turned toward the girls changing room, where I should have been all along, I guess.

This incident wasn't the first.

I was misgendered constantly as a kid. One time, a woman yelled at my mom in a public bathroom because her "son" was too old to come into the women's restroom. I didn't like when people thought I was a boy. It was less about their perception of my masculinity/androgyny and more about my lack of control over how others perceived and gendered me, something that confused my childhood brain and clouded my internal understanding of my gender. That night, I asked my mom if I could grow my hair long and get my ears pierced. I didn't want to be called a boy anymore; it didn't feel right.

It took over fifteen years to undo the damage of those days. I came out as queer in my early twenties, then as non-binary in my midtwenties, then as trans in my late twenties, and finally got top surgery a few months after my thirtieth birthday. I'm now in a place where I genuinely love my body and experience gender euphoria on a daily basis, but that wasn't true for the first three decades of my life. For many other queer and trans people, it can be far longer. Those trials and errors can have serious consequences. The only reason I'm not a part of the overwhelming statistics on LGBTQ+ youth suicide rates (don't worry, we'll get to that) is because I was *lucky*.

Despite growing up in Manhattan, one of the most diverse and open-minded places in the country, in an "accepting" family, we didn't have conversations about gender or sexuality when I was growing up, and I'm pretty sure my parents were just as confused about me as I was. I don't blame them because they simply didn't have the resources they needed to help me (like this book).

The fact of the matter is that regardless of how liberal or progressive my environment was growing up, I was still a queer and trans nonbinary kid coming of age in a rigidly heteronormative, binary-gendered world, and I saw no reflection of myself no matter where I looked. I knew gay people existed in the world. I saw men holding hands walking down the street in the West Village. I sneaked into R-rated screenings of *Brokeback Mountain* too many times to count. But all these examples did was illuminate the existence of gay people—and how hard queer existence can be; it didn't tell me what it means to be gay. I never once thought that because they existed, I could be a gay person, too. That I could even be a queer—let alone trans—kid.

Now that I'm finally living fully queerly as my trans nonbinary self, I'm finding happiness I never thought I was capable of feeling. It's euphoria, it's freedom, and it's a newfound strength, purpose, and confidence I've never felt. I own my mind and my body and my desires fully for the first time in my life without a single care for what anyone else might think about me. My initial coming out wasn't an event; it was a decision. A decision to live fully in my truth and to stop lying about who I am. And I've had to make that same decision over and over again in my life as I've continued along the path of self-discovery that I didn't have access to as a child. *Queer Kid Stuff* is the show I wish I'd had as a confused queer trans kid. This book is what I wish my parents had so they could have helped me along the way.

ON LANGUAGE: ESTABLISHING A BASELINE

Before we start getting into it all, it's important to first establish a baseline of knowledge so we can all dive into this work with shared language and understanding from the get-go. You're going to learn a lot of new vocabulary throughout this book! Some of it you might have heard before and some you might not. If you come across a word you're unfamiliar with or need a refresher on, you can use the robust index at the end of the book or just head over to handy-dandy Google and scour the internet for reliable queer-authored resources and glossaries. There are plenty of them, I promise! But there are also a few concepts you need to be familiar with before we get started.

You'll notice throughout the book that I use they/them pronouns quite a lot, particularly when I'm giving situational examples and hypotheticals where it's not necessary to use gendered language. Language around childhood is excruciatingly gendered, so I hope what I'm doing here will help you—consciously or unconsciously—become more aware of gendered language in your day-to-day lives!

You'll also notice that I don't use words like "homophobia," "transphobia," "biphobia," or other "phobia" words. Instead, I use the prefix "anti-." So instead of talking about homophobia, I'll say that someone or something is anti-gay. For transphobia, I'll use anti-trans. And you can keep shifting the -phobia framing to anti- for other forms of bigotry. I do this because "phobia," according to Merriam-Webster, is an exaggerated, disabling, inexplicable, or illogical fear. Fear is something that is a natural and rational part of the human experience, whereas the oppressive treatment of marginalized people is not "fear"; it is bigotry. I've shifted my language from "-phobia" to "anti-" to acknowledge that there is nothing natural or rational about any kind of bigotry.

Finally, let's get you up to speed on a more complex grown-up understanding of queerness. The word "queer" has many definitions and meanings, both personal and cultural, that are held individually. Here in this book, when I use the word "queer" I'm not usually using it as synonymous for "gay" or "homosexual" unless it's clearly indicated. When I use the word "queer" in this book, I'm talking about queer as a theoretical concept from the field of queer studies. Here, the word "queer" is charged. Queer not as in gay or homosexual but queer as in other, queer as in opposition to everything that is deemed "normal" by society and culture at large. It represents an oppositional (and even political) position that pushes against norms across both gender and sexuality. "Queer" pairs this oppositional and political definition with its cultural definition: simultaneously describing a larger community, because anyone who is not heterosexual and/or cisgender can be deemed queer and a part of the queer community. It's an *extremely* powerful word! I won't get too much more academic on you here, but I've always loved this quote from queer scholar Eve Kosofsky Sedgwick on queerness:

> *"Queer" can refer to: the open mesh of possibilities, gaps, overlaps, dissonances and resonances, lapses and excesses of meaning when the constituent elements of anyone's gender, of anyone's sexuality aren't made (or can't be made) to signify monolithically.*

The word "queer" contains multitudes. It is sexuality, it is gender, it is love, it is politic, it is opposition, it is rebellion, it is liberation, it is futurism, it is chaos, and it is joy. Sit with that a second, I know it's dense. Queer studies has deep roots in philosophy after all! If it's not quite clicking with you yet, don't worry; you'll get there! I encourage you to revisit Sedgwick's words if you're ever feeling lost—I know I certainly do.

A FEW NOTES . . .

. . . for Parents and Guardians

You are *the most* important person in your child's life—no pressure! Here's the good news: this book can stay with you and fold into your daily life. I know you're busy. You're probably juggling young kids plus a full-time job, plus household duties, and barely have a moment to tie your shoes. And I know there are a million and one parenting books that all claim that their way is the best way, but this isn't one of them. This is more than a book you just read; it's a book you live out. This is a book about nurturing and affirming identity, and the ground zero of identity work is in the home. What we are working on together is your ability to nurture the process of self-actualization, of coming of age. So, you can't leave the work of this book on the page, you have to bring it into your life and that means we're going to be doing a lot of deep, hard, and rewarding work together. Dig in deep, 'cause once you're in it, you're in it for good! Your homework assignment is to *do the work*.

. . . for Educators

You are the vanguard of this work. Most kids spend more time in classrooms than they do at home, but you already know that. You know the power you have over small minds, and you understand the responsibility that comes with it. Or at least I hope you do! If you've been nervous about bringing LGBTQ+ and social justice work into your classroom—no matter your subject or personal identity—I hope this book gives you courage. When you're writing lesson plans and coming up with activities, you might remember this book and remind yourself to include a blank space for pronouns next to "name" on a handout or worksheet or test. When a boy in your class starts wearing a dress to school, you might use the tools in this book to affirm his choice and have frank and open discussions about gender with your class. And when a narrow-minded school administrator or disgruntled parent asks you about your teaching methods, you can hand them this book so you don't have to do the work and expend the emotional labor yourself. I hope this book teaches you something, but I also hope it inspires you, because you inspire me. It's the least I can do for all that you do. Your homework assignment is to *keep going.*

. . . for Caregivers

I know you fill a funky space. You're not quite parent, you're not quite teacher. You don't have primary power in your kid's homelife or their education. I know because I've been one of you! I've nannied on and off throughout my adult life to make ends meet and have basically made a career out of being every kid's fun guncle.[4] What you do have is incredible *influence,* not only with the young people you work with but—maybe more importantly—with their parents. That influence can mean everything. The first queer person in

---

4 An affectionate term that shortens the phrase "gay uncle."

my life was my preschool teacher Cynthia, but I don't remember her because she was my teacher when I was three.
I remember her because she and her wife would babysit me
when my parents went out for date nights. The work of this
book for you is unique. It's a tool to teach and empower you
to do this direct work with young folks—like an educator
would. But you are also an important part of your charge's
self-realization and identity building in a way educators aren't
because they are not in the home. Support parents as they
do this work, ideally, alongside you. Do so with your safety
in mind, of course. If you are a queer or trans or Black, Indigenous, People of Color (BIPOC) caretaker, you should keep
your employment and safety at the fore. But if you have any
amount of privilege as a white straight cisgender person, then
you have to do the legwork with the parents you work with.
Your homework assignment is to *read this book and pass it on.*

Part I

THE STAKES

THE STATE OF LGBTQ+ YOUTH

Content Warning: youth suicide, anti-trans rhetoric, and legislation

Before we get into the work of spreading queer joy, you need to understand why this work is both incredibly important and incredibly urgent. I know you are committed to giving the kids in your care the best life you can—you're reading this book, after all—but I need to lay everything out to show how vital this work is, how vital it is that you integrate the lessons of this book into everything you do as soon as possible, and that this work is a constant, never-ending project. Take a deep breath and bear with me through this section. There's a lot to get through, and some of this might be hard to hear, but we have to get through the muck before we can reach the shore.

In December 2014, seventeen-year-old Leelah Alcorn in Lebanon, Ohio, left a note on her Tumblr specifically calling out her loss of hope as a young trans girl before she died by suicide as a result of her declining mental health.

In April 2019, fifteen-year-old Nigel Shelby in Huntsville, Alabama, died by suicide after being bullied for being gay.

In 2018, it was nine-year-old Jamel Myles in Denver, Colorado.

According to The Trevor Project's National Survey on LGBTQ Youth Mental Health in 2021, "42% of LGBTQ youth seriously considered attempting suicide in the past year, including more than half of transgender and nonbinary youth . . .

. . . 75% of LGBTQ youth reported that they had experienced discrimination based on their sexuality or gender identity at least once in their lifetime" while more than half had experienced discrimination in the past year.

"72% of LGBTQ youth reported symptoms of generalized anxiety in the past two weeks, including more than 3 in 4 transgender and nonbinary youth.

. . . 62% of LGBTQ youth reported symptoms of major depressive disorder in the past two weeks, including more than 2 in 3 transgender and nonbinary youth . . .

. . . 30% of LGBTQ youth experienced food insecurity in the past month, including half of all Native/Indigenous LGBTQ youth."

According to a recent study from the Chapin Hall at the University of Chicago, LGBTQ youth are 120 percent more likely to experience homelessness than non-LGBTQ youth. While an estimated 7 percent of youth identify as LGBTQ, 40 percent of unhoused youth identify as LGBTQ.

The Human Rights Campaign (HRC) marked 2021 as the deadliest year on record in their annual report on violence against transgender and gender nonconforming people in the United States. That report honors at least *forty-six* transgender and gender nonconforming people killed in 2021 alone. More than half of these victims were Black. Since January 2013, the HRC has documented more than 250 transgender and gender nonconforming people across 113 cities and 33 states who were violently murdered for being transgender or gender nonconforming.

As I write this, conservative legislatures in more than thirty states are working to pass anti-LGBTQ+ bills targeting trans and nonbinary youth's ability to use their school's bathroom, participate in after-school sports that align with their gender identity, and restrict their access to lifesaving gender-affirming healthcare. Ron DeSantis, Florida's current governor, passed the "Don't Say Gay" law through the state legislature that not only puts a blanket ban on any discussions of gender identity or sexuality in Florida schools up to the third grade but also requires teachers to out their queer, trans, and nonbinary students to their parents, endangering that child's safety and well-being at home.

These statistics and irrefutable facts about the state of LGBTQ youth are stark. They are difficult to stomach because they are true. The stories behind these statistics are not outliers, they are the norm. The only reason I didn't become a statistic is because I was lucky. I was an incredibly depressed and confused teenager. My declining mental health in my late teens led me to dangerous situations, substance abuse, and a sexual assault. The only reason I was able to pull myself up from rock bottom was because going away to college was a choice for me. So many do not have the privilege I had or access to wealth that is necessary for college to be an option. I made it through because I was *lucky*.

The mental health crisis for LGBTQ+ youth is so acute

that the United States has multiple large-scale organizations specifically dedicated to addressing the issue on a daily, even hourly, basis: The Trevor Project, Trans Lifeline, and the It Gets Better Project; local organizations, like the Ali Forney Center in New York City, that provide housing specifically for unhoused LGBTQ+ youth; and BIPOC-led organizations like The Okra Project and Black Trans Travel Fund that support queer and trans BIPOC, some of the most vulnerable in our community. We even have LGBTQ+ specific advocacy and legal organizations like Lambda Legal, and an entire gay and trans-focused department at the ACLU headed up by the incomparable Chase Strangio, that fight for LGBTQ+ rights in courtrooms across America. These organizations do vital work to support a community in the midst of crisis.

This is not meant to diminish the vital need for these organizations and their incredible work, but they are Band-Aids. They jump in to help queer folks who have already entered crisis mode; they do not prevent that crisis from taking root in the first place. Media organizations like GLAAD that advocate for proper LGBTQ+ representation in television and film are on the path to this prevention mission to shift culture, build empathy, and eventually eradicate anti-queer and anti-trans bigotry, but I believe that we need to invest in true intervention. I'm talking about reaching young kids through education, and representation specifically in children's media, including preschool television. I believe this tactic, based in early childhood media and education, will significantly improve the well-being of the LGBTQ+ community as a whole, working as a preventative strategy for healing our collective crisis. Not only will it cultivate affirmed LGBTQ+ kids and kids from LGBTQ+ families, but it will reach further in creating meaningful allies in their straight and cisgender peers—those who might otherwise perpetrate harm by parroting anti-trans and anti-queer societal biases.

Research shows that even a little bit of support and acceptance in a young LGBTQ+ person's life can have a significant positive impact on their mental health and bring down the likelihood of attempting suicide. The Trevor Project's 2021 National Survey on LGBTQ Youth Mental Health found that transgender and nonbinary youth who said that the people they live with respect their pronouns attempted suicide at half the rate of those whose pronouns weren't respected. That's a HUGE difference! And! A new report from the American Academy of Pediatrics and TransYouth Project found that five years after transitioning, only 2.5 percent of the trans kids they followed re-transitioned to the gender they were assigned at birth. Trans kids know themselves better than you might think!

It took me years to sort through and undo the various internalized prejudices that led to preventable traumas in my adolescence. Queer, trans, and nonbinary people like me, and many more with far less privilege than I have, are struggling against the oppression of a binary cisgender and straight-centered capitalist world. It is killing and traumatizing too many of us. We are your friends, we are your neighbors, we are your siblings, your students, and *your children*. Even if you or your kids don't currently identify as queer or trans, it is incredibly likely that someone around you identifies somewhere under the LGBTQ+ umbrella. Maybe there's a queer student in your child's class; maybe one of your students is closeted or comes from a same-sex parent household; maybe it's your cousin or your child's best friend's sibling. Statistically speaking, queer and trans people are everywhere! And we need you to care about us because the systems we live in sure don't.

It's taken me nearly two decades to undo my own internalized anti-gay and anti-trans beliefs ingrained in me through the trauma of constant misgendering and not having the language or support system to combat those questions as I was developing my sense of self. I struggled that much and for that long even though I come from an "accepting and liberal family." If it's taken someone like me—with a heck of a lot of privilege and support from my well-meaning, if occasionally obtuse, family—this long to figure things out, I can only think of the young people who aren't so lucky. You don't have to follow that train of thought much further to understand why the suicide and houseless rates in LGBTQ+ youth are still so high. The obstacles we face are daunting.

My solution is to generate and distribute the resources that I lacked as a child. I want to give today's youngest the language and education and stories to sort through their identities, develop confidence and a vocabulary to communicate that identity to the world while developing an abundant capacity for empathy. But in order to reach a necessary critical mass to truly make a difference on a large, even global scale, I need your help.

I have a strategy for how we can start to make things better, but I can't do it alone. Let's spread queer joy.

THE OBSTACLES AHEAD

This path hasn't been an easy one, that's for sure. I started coming up against gatekeepers early on in my career, before it even truly started. Those experiences were incredibly difficult, I won't sugarcoat it. There aren't a lot of people who also do what I do and there's a reason: it is *incredibly* difficult. The spaces where you can make this work can concurrently be actively hostile to it. There are dissenting voices coming from every corner, it's not particularly lucrative, and it's frustrating to shout something so important into the void and get no acknowledgment or response back. But even though the dissenting voices have gate kept these spaces for a long time, they continue to recycle old arguments that are starting to go stale. My very first experience with a gatekeeper happened when I was in college and gave me a crash course in the anti-queer and anti-trans obstacles and stigmas to come. So let's revisit that gatekeeper to take a look at what happened and use those dissensions to figure out how we can combat our own internal biases and build a strategy to destabilize these obstacles.

WHEN THEY SHUT YOU DOWN

In undergrad, I fell into two passions: theater for young audiences (TYA) and gender studies. I took TYA and queer theory in the same quarter when I was at Northwestern, and I wondered why I couldn't put the philosophy I was learning to the craft I was cultivating. I wanted to smush queerness and storytelling for kids together—because, I mean, why not? But when I looked around, I saw that those stories I wanted to be a part of were few and far between. Most of the plays were for teens, and there were exactly two scripts[5]

---

5 They are *The Transition of Doodle Pequeño* by Gabriel Jason Dean (that I'll get into in a moment), and a still unpublished stage version of the popular picture book *And Tango Makes Three* by Justin Richardson and Peter Parnell called *And Then Came Tango* adapted by Emily Freeman. By the age of twenty-five, I had already directed productions of both these plays at Northwestern and the New York Fringe Festival.

written for middle and elementary school audiences. But most of the stories I encountered were written by white straight cisgender allies.

One of those plays was called *The Transition of Doodle Pequeño* by Gabriel Jason Dean. Directing that play my senior year would shape what I would later turn into a career and lifelong mission. It tells the story of a young undocumented boy nicknamed Doodle who recently moved into a new neighborhood with his mother on Halloween. He quickly meets one of his neighbors, Reno, who is a boy who loves to wear dresses and first enters the story wearing a bright pink tutu for Halloween. Doodle and Reno learn to put aside their differences in lieu of a blossoming friendship. It depicts the journey of a young gender nonconforming boy and his friend coming into allyship. It also tells a story of a neighborhood bully who is hiding secrets of her own and her little brother who doesn't know any better. The play as a whole is a beautiful script with a lovely message—you'd wonder why it was so controversial.

Our little production of *Doodle* was meant to tour the local Evanston, Illinois school district. The scrappy student-led children's theater board that produced the show—Purple Crayon Players (PCP)—booked us at three local elementary and middle schools. I, along with the cast and crew, got up early to pack up our set made of flimsy cardboard boxes, squish it into two vans, and ride off to our first school. We unloaded and set everything up in the auditorium and waited for the kids to come. Once our young audience assembled, we launched into our preshow workshop. We asked them questions to help introduce concepts from the play and used audience engagement and creative drama techniques to bring them into the world of the show. When we asked kids if they knew what "gay" meant, we got a few shocked looks (and surprised smiles) from teachers, but the kids' hands immediately shot up into the air with correct—not derogatory—answers.

When we met Reno about ten minutes into the play, I remember watching a teacher leave the auditorium with a scowl on her face. She returned a few scenes later with the principal in tow, who beelined to me and my tour managers. Keep in mind that there was no backstage. We were in an elementary school auditorium that had seats and a cleared area for the play. When she approached me, I was mere feet away from the performers mid-scene. As Reno faced his bullies, I faced my first in a very long line of gatekeepers. The principal asked us if we were promoting cross-dressing and drag, and that she couldn't have this. "What will the parents say?!"

I kept a calm head in a storm and was able to convince her to take this conversation to her office once the show was over. One of my tour managers and I made our way to her office during the postshow talkback and what preceded was a highlight reel of the conversations I've seen play out over and over again in response to my work over the better part of a decade. "This is not appropriate for young children," "What am I going to say when parents start calling my office?," and the one that stood out most to me at the time: "We don't even teach them about reproduction until the seventh grade."

I don't think we were able to sway her bigoted bias in that high-pressure situation, but she was able to needle out of us—the naive college students that we were—the name of the second school on our touring schedule. I left that first school simply glad that we'd been able to bring our queer little play to its intended young audience. But in the coming weeks, I'd be singing a different tune. The next school on our list sent an email. I never saw the exchange itself, but I knew they were asking questions about the age appropriateness of the play. They were getting cold feet. We answered their questions with transparency and referred back to the initial emails they sent when they originally booked the show.

But despite everyone's best efforts, the second school canceled our performance. My heart fell through my stomach. I think I kicked a rock or yelled or broke a wooden plank or something cliché like that when I heard the news. It was visceral. I went home that night and sobbed to my roommates. I could feel the weight of these gatekeepers pushing me out and locking the door behind me. I cared deeply about the performance because I cared deeply about the audience that was there to watch it. This cancellation was not about a performance that would never play; it was about the audience kept from seeing it. We went to only one local middle school after that, but then it was all over.

In that same theater for young audiences class, my professor snagged us a copy of Sarah Gubbins's unpublished play, *fml: how Carson McCullers saved my life,* about a teenage lesbian who copes with her bullies by drawing a comic book version of herself. We read scenes from the script in class and I volunteered to read the lead, Jo. I looked up after we read the pivotal scene where she comes out and faces her bullies, and my professor's face was streaming with tears. It was a transformative moment for me. I read that script and thought, if I had seen that play when I was an angsty confused teen, maybe I wouldn't have had so much internal struggle. Maybe it wouldn't have been so hard for me to understand myself because it was reflected back at me from a stage, through the powerful medium of story.

I saw my younger self, Little Lindz, for the first time that day. The kid in the photograph with a bowl cut and an ear-to-ear grin in their favorite pair of green corduroy overalls in front of hydrangeas bigger than their head who didn't care what anyone thought. That is me as my authentic self, and I saw that I had been running away from them all these years because I was scared. I thought of those kids who could have met Reno that day, and I cried. I cried because I knew there were kids at that school who might have seen themselves in Reno. I cried because they didn't get to feel seen that day, as they should have been. And I cried because I know how truly painful it can be to remain unseen. I thought what difference that one performance could have made on one life and I was mad. I knew this moment was the beginning of not only my career but a movement.

But there was a problem. I discovered that not only were plays written for young audiences with LGBTQ+ themes and characters few and far between but the ones that did exist were rarely, if ever, published, let alone produced by theaters or allowed in schools. I grew increasingly frustrated and graduated with a looming question around what my career might look like in this particular artistic pursuit.

Looking back at this formative pre-career experience, I can see where the obstacles I would soon come up against were powerfully foreshadowed. People are scared of this work. It is so deeply stigmatized that putting queer bodies and queer stories in front of children can send adults into a tailspin in full view of a packed auditorium. This early experience with one terrified principal was far from singular—it was indicative of every conversation I have had with naysayers for the better part of a decade. It showed me that my path forward was not only untrod, it was up a treacherous cliff face. The barriers I've faced are steeped in internalized anti-queer and anti-trans bigotry, even if these gatekeepers don't think their bigotry is explicit and probably, when prompted, would deny their biases.

These gatekeepers are the greatest hurdles along the mission to spread queer joy and they must be dismantled swiftly. In order to move forward and progress in this work, we must confront our own unconscious biases and help others work through theirs. This work is not easy, it can be excruciating, but it is more than necessary if we are to move toward a better world for queer folks. In other words, it's a good thing I like to rock climb.

WHAT IS CHILDISM?

The principal at the school during our tour of *Doodle* is a glimpse of the obstacles you might encounter on your journey, so we're going to dive in and face what stands in our way and how we can accomplish this massive mission. While a lot of these obstacles are imposed upon us by others (like the principal), I faced a lot of internalized biases that stood in my way. I'll address a few specific biases that I've encountered consistently as I've gone about this work, but ultimately it all boils down to internalized anti-gay, anti-queer, and anti-trans ideas, combined with childism.

Childism is a fairly new term for a very old idea. The late scholar and psychotherapist Elisabeth Young-Bruehl defined the term in her book *Childism: Confronting Prejudice Against Children*. Basically, childism is the unfair treatment of children because they are children, and not thought of as autonomous (tiny) humans with their own needs, desires, identity, and values outside of the expectations of adults. It sits snuggly between racism, anti-transness, anti-gayness, and all the other antis and isms, but is still largely unrecognized.

Acknowledging childism means affirming that children deserve to be seen as whole humans, with wants and needs of their own, and that they should be treated with respect. The best writing I've ever seen explaining childism (particularly to parents) comes from a poem called "On Children" written by the Lebanese-American poet Kahlil Gibran (1883–1931):

Your children are not your children.
They are the [children] of Life's longing for itself.
They come through you but not from you,
And though they are with you yet they belong not
to you.

Our children "come through [us]" but they are full and whole human beings in their own rights with thoughts and feelings and opinions and experiences that are separate from yours, and they should be treated and nurtured with that understanding. Parents, educators, and caregivers cannot dictate or shape who a child is or will become, they can only guide them along the way. It's when we grown-ups forget to look at children as whole people unto themselves and outside of *ourselves* that issues arise.

The roots of the largest obstacles in our work together form when childism couples with anti-trans, anti-queer, and anti-gay beliefs. This is how we end up with waves of anti-trans legislation specifically targeting trans kids' access to gender-affirming healthcare, athletics, and bathrooms. The conservative anti-LGBTQ+ "agenda" pivoted toward "protecting kids" after marriage equality passed into federal law through the Supreme Court. First, they went after gender-neutral bathrooms in schools; you might remember Gavin Grimm's case, *Grimm v. Gloucester County School Board*. Grimm came out as a transgender boy at his middle school, and his school responded by adopting a discriminatory new policy that kept boys and girls "with gender identity issues" from using the same restrooms as their classmates, specifically targeting Grimm. After four years of litigation with the ACLU, which included a trip to the Supreme Court, Grimm finally won his case, which was further affirmed in the court of appeals in the summer of 2020. After losing that battle, conservative politics pivoted again. This time, they specifically targeted trans kids by proposing state legislation across the country that prohibit trans youth from accessing gender-affirming healthcare like hormone blockers, and mandating that young trans athletes can only compete as the gender they were assigned at birth. Even moving toward prohibiting transgender *adults* from gender-affirming healthcare, forcing them to go off their prescribed hormones and detransition to the gender they were assigned at birth.

Bills like this aim to "protect children," or rather, to "protect childhood innocence." If I had a penny for every time

someone told me to "let kids be kids," I'd be Scrooge Mc-
Duck swimming in a private lake of golden coins. Let me tell
you a secret: there's no such thing as childhood innocence!
Or, at least not in the way you might understand it. It's childism enforced through a disguise, because it's far more sub-
tle than outright abuse or negligence. It's made up to keep
children from knowledge that would give them power and
agency and autonomy over their bodies and their selves.

Now, I'm not saying that we should show preschoolers
porn or videos of genocide, police brutality, or sexual violence. That will traumatize them unnecessarily because they
don't have the cognitive ability to process that information
in a healthy way. What I'm saying is that you *can* talk to kids
about pretty much anything—including genocide and other
difficult topics—when you approach them in a way that a
child can understand and digest. We shouldn't be shy about
talking to kids about important topics in order to "preserve
their childhood innocence." On the contrary, we should
make a concerted effort to talk to kids, even preschool-age
kids, about important *human* issues in a way that makes
sense to their brain developmentally. We'll discuss this more
in-depth when we talk about age-relevant sex and health education for preschoolers, but instead of traumatizing kids
with images of sexual violence, we can talk to them about
consent, body agency, and privacy in a way that helps protect
them from sexual predators. This is work of self-realization,
but it's also the work of abuse prevention. We want to protect children from trauma because they are *vulnerable*, not
because they are innocent.

We grown-ups so often forget what it was like to be kids.
Because of this, we make mistakes and often do things for

children "for their own good" without their consent, and without giving them the information and knowledge to make these choices for themselves. The biggest difference between a kid and a grown-up is lived experience. That's it! Toddlers and preschoolers are brand-new to the world. When they see, hear, touch, taste, smell, or generally experience something, they are probably doing so for the very first time. It's easy for grown-ups to forget seemingly small firsts like this when we were so new to the world. That's why we have to remember to go under the doorknob! Experiencing something, anything, for the first time is a big deal! It colors your perception of that thing or experience for a long time, if not the rest of your life. If you had a bad first experience with an apple, let's say, when you were a toddler, it's very likely that you wouldn't eat apples at all after that, or at least into adolescence or early adulthood. The difference in lived experience means that kids haven't experienced the world yet in the same way adults have. But that doesn't mean that they aren't still whole humans. They simply lack context, knowledge, and personal experience. And the lived experience they do have has an enormous impact on their development. So many grown-ups treat kids like they can't make decisions for themselves, when they are fully capable of doing so *if they are given the information they need to make that decision.*

In most households, a Black, Native, Brown, Latine, or Asian child will have considerably different conversations and experiences around race with their families than their white peers because of the privileges and lack thereof afforded to them by their race. For instance, while diverse children's media representation of race is *very slowly* getting better, it's far more likely that a white child will continually see themselves represented through white protagonists on their favorite television show. The representation and knowledge currently available to most children is incredibly narrow, predominantly reflecting cisgender white children from heterosexual familial structures.

All kids need access to a far more diverse representation and information that both reflects their own experiences outside of normative definitions and represents experiences that are different from their own.[6] There are so many differences that kids can experience that include racial differences, gender, sexuality, family structures, neurodivergences, disability, socioeconomic status, the list goes on. Some of these differences might even be invisible, like mental health. There is no way to know which kids need what resources, so they *all* need to get *all* of them. We'll get into the differences between *equality, equity,* and *justice* in a later chapter, but we can think of scaffolding our discussions with kids in this way as they grow. Starting with equality: educating all kids equally across representations and possibilities for identities. Then shifting to equity: placing emphasis on identities and experiences that are systemically oppressed. And moving into justice: looking at ways to recognize and build systems that are inherently unbiased.

I'm asking what the world would look like if all kids had access to all the information they need for themselves and to uplift and affirm and support and be allies to others. That's

---

6 If we really want to get into it, I consider *all kids queer.* Queer as in pre-structural. Queer as in different. Queer as in outside of the narrative centered by society that prioritizes white cisgender straight male *adults.*

what letting all "kids be kids" looks like to me, and that's
what we're trying to achieve. We have to let kids be kids in
a way that encompasses *all kids.*

WORKING THROUGH OUR BIASES

You might be wondering: Why so young? Why should we
have conversations with little kids about gender and sexuality? Why can't we talk to them about it when they are older,
when it's more relevant? Let's put a pin in the unconscious
bias (or implicit bias—subconsciously held social stereotypes)
of our question for a moment to provide some semblance of
an answer. The short answer is that any later is too late. The
long answer is that preschoolers in particular are at the age
when we begin to develop our sense of self and our identities
in relation to the world around us.

We've talked about the importance of specifically targeting early childhood spaces with queer education, but we
haven't talked about why I am constantly bombarded with
this question in the first place. That's because of stigma and
internal bias, and no matter who you are, I guarantee you
have both around queerness and children. It took me nearly
two decades to sort through mine and I'm *still* working
through some of it. We all have some form of internalized
anti-queer, anti-gay, anti-trans biases because the world we
live in bombards us with those sentiments, whether that's
conscious or unconscious. So we're going to name and try to
dismantle some of the commonly held stigmas and unconscious biases specifically around queerness and kids that you
probably hold. It might get a little uncomfortable, but this is
the necessary work we have to do to rebuild how we think
about these topics and approach them with the young people
in our lives. First, we have to discuss cognitive identity de-

velopment theory; that's the fancy academic way of talking about how we develop an understanding of our identity.

I've already mentioned that the biggest cognitive difference between kids and grown-ups is lived experience. Kids come into the world without context! They gather information through their senses, process all of that information, and make sense of it. Young children are like tiny sponges. They observe and experiment with the world around them in order to understand how it functions on multiple levels. My wife and I were on a call with a family friend who had had her baby a few months before, and every time she tried to talk, he would stick his hand in her mouth. He was trying to figure out where the sound of her voice was coming from!

Toddlers follow their instincts. They test their physical boundaries, they experiment with behavior, they mimic, and they observe. When I trained to become a family music teacher, we learned that some kids might actively participate in class and grab instruments and sing along, but others might sit quietly the entire class without making a peep. My mom brought me to Music Together classes when I was a toddler, and I was that shy quiet kid who hid under the table in the corner. But neither of these behaviors are bad. A few years later I started singing around the house, and I haven't stopped since. Even when you think a kid isn't listening, absorbing, or learning, they usually are in a more profound way than you might imagine.

There are plenty of parenting books that detail developmental milestones for your child—when they start communicating, talking, crawling, cruising, standing, walking, etc. We understand these milestones because they indicate success, but we rarely look at the actual developmental process behind them—how kids absorb and process information (input) to be able to put something of their own out into the world (output). While kids are learning to walk and talk, they are also learning behavior, social cues, and so much more about their immediate environments. Not only are they dealing with all of this external information hitting them all at once and attempting to parse through it, they are also dealing with their own internal systems like learning how to regulate their emotions and recognize a want or a need and communicate it clearly. All of that is a lot of work! So next time your toddler throws a tantrum, pause for a second and think what it must be like to attempt to function like a human being with all of that (waves hands around) happening inside.

The late Susan Harter, a professor and scholar in psychology, wrote about the process behind self-development in her book *The Construction of the Self: Developmental and Sociocultural Foundations*. Not to get too academic on you here, but basically Harter says that we understand the world around us through both our understanding of ourselves and our relationships to those around us. This part about our relationships is so important, and this is where you come in if you are a parent or guardian, because what relationships are most influential to a child and their development? Their family, however that family might be made up! Everything you do teaches them about how the world works and who they are within it.

If we go back to the idea that kids are tiny sponges, then we need to think hard about what exactly kids are soaking up, and who gets to make decisions about their environment that dictates what they are soaking up. In most cases, those decision makers are, first, family members, the most important grown-ups in their lives, and later, educators.

What does all that have to do with gender and sexuality?

Well, I'm glad you asked, because it has *everything* to do with gender and sexuality. At the same time a toddler is developing the skills to walk and talk, they are also beginning to form an understanding of their identity and of themselves in relation to the world around them. Just like they listen to the people around them talk in order to begin to form words themselves, they watch and observe the dynamics and behaviors of those around them in order to form their identity.

Let's use gender as an example. An adult has a fully formed understanding of gender as a concept, based both on their own lived experience and how they were raised to think about gender. Most of today's adults were raised thinking about gender along the binary of:

man | woman
boy | girl
male | female
masculine | feminine

These adults were raised believing their own gender must fall on one side of the binary, tied inextricably to the gender they were assigned at birth by a doctor. Each gender comes with its own set of rules, norms, stereotypes, and privileges (or lack thereof). Most grown-ups grew up in a world with a bias toward binary, cisgendered, straight, white people. Most doctors and parents assume that a fetus with a vagina is a girl.[7] The baby is born, and they stick an *F* on their birth certificate that will stay with them through the rest of their life. The

---

7 There are actual measurements that doctors use to determine the "normative" length for a baby's penis or clitoris to determine whether they are male, female, or intersex.

doctor and parents in this situation *might* be correct, but they also might not be! If that assumption is correct, that's great, that kid is *lucky* that the gender assigned to them based on their genitalia was correct. They are coming into a world as a cisgender kid whose gender identity is reflected back to them in a positive light because it is the gender identity that is centered in modern culture. Trans and nonbinary kids don't have that privilege.

Adults have walked through their lives experiencing byproducts of the gender binary every day, from how they dress and present themselves to the world, to how they interact with others in groups, in professional spaces, and in romantic and sexual relationships, to how they are treated by others and by society at large. An adult's idea of gender is not only their literal understanding of the concept but also foundational to the way our world functions and how they have lived so far within that system. In a nutshell, adults approach concepts like gender with a whole lot of baggage.

Kids, in particular preschoolers, have few preconceived notions or lived experiences. They are new to our world and its machinations. They are tabula rasa,[8] a blank slate, at least as far as culture goes. They are uninitiated in our current societal understanding of gender because that understanding is not innate, it's not something we are born understanding because it's a *social construct*. Human concepts like race and gender are *social constructs*.

Everything we hold dear in our society was, at some point, made up and then collectively agreed upon as factual and true. Social constructs range from rules of etiquette, to

---

8 Not trying to get into an argument about existential philosophy here, just illustrating a point!

applying value to a piece of paper and calling it a dollar bill, to the way we categorize fruits versus vegetables, to how we count and organize the passage of time, to our modern conception of gender. For example, we have universally, as a human society, agreed that an apple is a fruit because we have decided that any edible fleshy food that comes from a tree or plant and contains seeds is a fruit. And we have decided that broccoli is a vegetable because it is part of a plant that can be used as food. But what if we had decided something different? What if we said that only foods that were round were fruits and everything else was a vegetable? Then pears would be vegetables and Brussels sprouts would be fruit! Welcome to the Matrix, folks.

Not only do kids not yet have a solid definition of the social construct of gender, but they also don't yet have an internalized concept of what their *own* gender is. Children, in this way, are impressionable. Their understanding and exploration of gender at this point in their lives will greatly affect their future, because their spongy little brains are absorbing. They explore the physical structures of the world while they, in tandem, observe the intangible structures—our social constructs. When a four-year-old sees a (probably trans or nonbinary) person with a beard wearing a dress, they might ask you, "Why is that man wearing a dress?" That child is actively grappling with their internal conception of gender. By that point they have learned that women and girls wear dresses and men and boys do not. Men (and some boys) have facial hair and women and girls do not. Seeing a person with a beard (a male characteristic) who is also wearing a dress (a female characteristic) does not align with the gender construct they have come to understand. It's so much easier to construct a child's understanding of gender that includes trans, nonbinary, and gender nonconforming identities and expressions before it becomes reinforced and rigid along binary gender. Don't worry, we'll get deeper into how we can do that later.

The actual teachable information we provide to young children is important, but what might be even more impressionable is their environment. If a child hears their parents say racist things, they are more likely to parrot them, believe those notions themselves, and internalize and later perpetuate systemic racism. The same cycle goes for gender and sexuality. This process might be subtler—for example, making the automatic assumption that your child might be straight and cisgender before they have the communication tools to tell you otherwise. While this assumption might not be outwardly anti-gay or anti-trans, its impact can be gargantuan to a small child who is beginning to formulate their identity. When you shed so much light on one thing, everything around it must become darker. Where cisness is visible, transness is invisible. Where cisness knows no obstacles, transness becomes one obstacle after another: from self-actualizing to coming out to changing your legal name and gender marker on your passport, driver's license, health insurance, credit cards to getting approval for hormones and surgery to change your own body to daily microaggressions and misgendering. The difference between the experience of a cis person versus a trans person is HUGE! And that enormous contrast trickles down to individual thoughts, opinions, and preconceived notions.

Remember that a child's introduction to the world around them comes through you, an unreliable narrator, with your own thoughts, opinions, and preconceived notions and biases about pretty much everything. It doesn't matter if you consider yourself an "ally." It doesn't even matter if you are queer or trans yourself! No matter who you are, you have, over the course of your lived experience of the world, soaked up and internalized—like the tiny sponge you once were—all of these thoughts, opinions, and preconceived notions and they have, to some extent, become your own. If you, as a grown-up in a young person's life, are producing thoughts, and opinions, and preconceived notions, then you are actively passing them along. And I get it. This work is really hard! You have to rewire your brain to disrupt these vicious cycles, but I promise you can.

The first step is recognizing this cycle. We can preemptively disrupt our own biased thoughts, opinions, and preconceived notions so that we can be purposeful in the information that we provide to young people through our words, actions, behaviors, and environments so that they can soak up information that decidedly does not center cisness and straightness and whiteness. While we can't isolate kids in a world where that dynamic doesn't exist, we can strive toward providing them with an ideal, give them the tools to recognize bias at an age-relevant level, and teach them to question the world as it is presented to them. We can do the work of making a better world as grown-ups, but we can't forget to talk to the kids in our lives about these issues. How else will they bring about a better world for themselves as they develop and gain power and autonomy?

All this to say that the reason why we have to talk to young kids about gender and sexuality and race and class and so many other things that intimately impact our identities is because any later is too late.

THE FOUR MOST COMMON STIGMAS

Since that production of *Doodle* was canceled, I've run into a whole lot of other gatekeepers and dissenters from all over the world. And even though I do my best not to read the comments,[9] I've noticed a few patterns. Beyond your run-of-the-mill internet troll and Russian bot, there are four common stigmas around queerness and children that come up over and over again in response to my work. They are that I'm (1) sexualizing children, (2) turning kids gay—tagging along on the assumption that (3) being gay is a choice or disease—and that I'm (4) brainwashing kids. Let's debunk these stigmas, shall we!

Stigma #1: "You're Sexualizing Children."

This one is tricky, because it is mostly born out of confusion, and a lack of proper knowledge and education around sexuality. There are two assumptions happening here: (1) that talking about sexuality with children necessarily sexualizes children and (2) that sexuality cannot be separated from sex. These assumptions are *not* true. Talking to kids about sexuality in fact does not sexualize them and you can *absolutely* talk about sexuality without talking about sex.

Saying that this work sexualizes children implies that children are the object being sexualized. Sexualizing someone means that we are turning them into an object of someone's sexual attraction and that they are sexually desired. When an adult sexualizes kids, that is pedophilia. I have been called this over and over again because of my work; I must have about fifty different spellings of the words "pedophile" and "groomer" on the block list for the *Queer Kid Stuff* YouTube

---

9 Never, ever, *ever* read the comments!

channel. This is because people think that talking to kids about queerness and gender and sexuality means you are talking to them about queer sex, which is misleading.

The root of the issue here is that most people equate discussions of sexuality with discussions around sex, and specifically intercourse. But that's not necessarily the case—sexuality, or the gender(s) a person is attracted to, is not the same thing as the act of sex. They are connected, sure, but sex is only one very small part of what sexuality is, and that means you don't have to understand sex to understand sexuality.

When I talk to preschoolers about sexuality, I use concepts they are already familiar with: gender and love and family. Sex and intercourse are completely separate conversations, because it's not relevant at their age. When I spoke with sex and health educator Justine Ang Fonte, she reminded me that we have to make sure we are answering the question the child is really asking. If they want to know where babies come from, you can speak scientifically about eggs, sperm, and uteri. If they want to know what gay means, you can talk about boys who love boys and girls who love girls. Most kids honestly don't care about sex and probably aren't interested in it in the first place! Those conversations can happen when they are older and it becomes more relevant to their lives as they reach puberty.

The bias that talking about sexuality to kids sexualizes them comes from the hyper-sexualization of queerness, as well as the leftover cultural stigma from the HIV/AIDS pandemic that has trickled down to today's perception of the LGBTQ+ community. Queerness is extricable from queer sex, *and* queer sex isn't evil. (The idea that queer sex is evil can be traced back to anti-sodomy laws and Christian-based anti-gay dogma. The Supreme Court only ruled in 2003 in

Lawrence v. Texas that anti-sodomy laws are unconstitutional. That was not very long ago.) However, the stigma that conflates queerness with queer sex is complicated and fraught with anti-queer bias, but the fact is queer sex is one part of a much, much larger queer culture, and conflating the two erases everything else that makes up our queerness, and turns our identities into something that is considered taboo. (We also need to do the work to wash away the stigma around queer sex itself, but that's not the work of this particular book.)

Talking about sexuality doesn't necessitate discussions of sex and neither does talking more specifically about queer sexuality. Because we can talk about sexuality by talking about gender and love and family, that means that we can talk about queer sexuality through gender and love and family, too! This doesn't give you an out on talking about sex with young kids—that's also a very important conversation, but they are separate, so this shouldn't be the sticking point that keeps you from talking about sexuality with young kids.

The truth of the matter is that this work is active abuse prevention. Talking to kids about sexuality gives them the tools and confidence of knowledge to protect themselves from potential abuse from sexual predators. We'll dig deeper into that in later chapters but just know that these conversations are *extremely* important!

Giving a child knowledge about sexuality is not the same as telling a child that they have a certain sexuality. I am not prescribing any kind of sexuality for a child. That is for them to discover on their own as they develop their own flavor of sexual and romantic attraction growing up, including discovering they don't experience some kinds of attraction at all, in the case of some asexual identities. Kids need access to knowledge in order to make those discoveries on their own terms. You have the ability to empower them with knowledge through conversations about all possibilities for their potential sexuality without skewing the information or assuming they fall under one sexuality or another before they can explore those questions safely for themselves.

Stigma #2: "You're Turning Kids Gay/Trans."

Queer and trans grown-ups were once queer and trans kids. I didn't come out until my twenties, but I was queer and trans before I came out. I was queer and trans when I was a teen, I was queer and trans when I was a tween, and I was queer and trans when I was a toddler, too.

These fundamental aspects of a person's identity do not typically change. We make new discoveries about ourselves, and our capacity for fluidity in our identity might shift, but a queer or trans person has always been queer or trans. There is no such thing as turning someone gay. In a massive 2019 study published in *Science,* scientists finally debunked the existence of a "gay gene." They found that human DNA cannot predict an individual's sexuality. Human sexuality cannot be pinned down by biology, psychology, or life experiences alone because all three are equally important. Human sexuality is complex and cannot be explained by only one of these factors.

All I am doing is providing the knowledge and representation that is necessary for someone to make discoveries about themselves. What I do might trigger a lightbulb moment for a queer or trans kid that will help them understand and unlock the mystery of self at an earlier age. That doesn't mean we're turning *someone* into *something*. If anything, it's helping young people come into themselves younger, which means fewer years of confusion and fewer years of struggle and trauma. That is not the same as turning someone gay.

There's a reason why one of every six Gen Zers identify as queer or transgender![10]

Let's look at the history of left-handedness, for example.[11] The scientist and researcher Dr. Chris McManus found that there has been a significant increase in left-handedness over the last one hundred years. Left-handedness didn't get trendier; what changed was we stopped pressuring kids to be right-handed. It is no longer shameful to be a lefty so more and more people who are naturally left-handed are living their best lefty lives. Take it from my lefty mom *and* mother-in-law! Similarly, statistics coming from Gen Z don't reflect queerness or transness as trendy. It's simply becoming less shameful and more openly accepted for people to be queer or trans, so more and more people who are *naturally* queer or trans are openly identifying in that way. Just like lefties!

Just as there have always been lefties, there have always been trans kids. I think it's really easy to fall into the trap of assuming that the existence of trans and nonbinary kids is something new. But that's not true. There have always been (and there always will be) trans kids! Trans historian Jules Gill-Peterson went deep into the archives for her seminal book, *Histories of the Transgender Child,* where she painstakingly details a recorded history of transgender kids throughout the twentieth century starting in the early 1900s. The book refutes the claim that transgender kids "have no history, that they are fundamentally new and somehow, therefore deserving of less than human recognition." Gill-

---

10 Jones, Jeffrey M. "LGBT Identification Rises to 5.6% in Latest U.S. Estimate," Gallup Inc., accessed January 10, 2023, https://www.gallup .com/corporate/212381/who-we-are.aspx.

11 Author Julia Serano first popularized this argument!

Peterson asserts that "we don't know trans children because we have inherited, reinforced, and perpetuated a cultural system of gender and childhood in which they are unknowable." So throw away the notion that trans kids are a *new* phenomenon because trans kids have always been here. We just haven't known how to be there *for them*—until now!

I had the pleasure of talking to Dr. Jason Rafferty, a pediatrician and psychiatrist who specializes in a gender-affirming healthcare model for queer and trans youth. With the parents of the children in his care, "early recognition and early support is essential, but [he thinks] it's also scary," mostly because there is a huge lack of proper information out there. In his gender-affirming model there is "no desired outcome. It's not about turning people trans, it really is about accepting each and every person for who they are and providing a different, additional support if needed along that journey." We are not turning kids into anything, we are nurturing their growth and ability to self-determine these sides of their identities.

Stigma #3: "It's a Choice/Disease."

When I spoke further with Dr. Rafferty, he told me about the four accepted premises of the gender-affirmative pediatric care he specializes in, which you can remember regardless of whether or not your kid is queer and/or trans:

1. Transgender identity and diverse gender expressions do *not* constitute a mental health disorder.
2. Variations in gender identity and expression are normal aspects of human diversity, and binary definitions of gender do not always reflect emerging gender identities.

3. Gender identity involves an interplay between biology, development, socialization, and culture.

4. If a mental health issue exists, it most often stems from stigma and negative experiences, rather than being intrinsic to the person.

I think these are important baseline tenets to remember when we talk about queer and trans people, especially young ones. The stigma that talking to kids about gender and sexuality leads them to make a choice to be queer or trans is a bias that's less targeted at me and is more of an underlying misunderstanding of queerness, particularly transness. Queerness and transness are neither a choice, nor are they a disease. This is a scientific truth! Yes, many queer and trans people and youth have mental illness, but that mental illness is not their queerness and/or transness itself.

Mental illness comes about in many different ways for many different people, but mental illness that is connected to queerness and transness has to do with the outside forces at play telling queer people that they're unlovable or when trans people can't express their gender because they don't feel safe. The Trevor Project's 2021 survey found that 70 percent of LGBTQ youth had "poor" mental health during the COVID-19 pandemic, showing how a queer or trans person's mental health status has more to do with circumstances than how a young person might identify. For example, a trans teen who was able to be out and open about their gender at school in 2019 would likely have declining mental health during a pandemic where they are forced to stay at home in an environment that does not allow them to express their gender authentically.

So, break down any assumptions you might have around

queerness and transness and mental illness and remember
that gender and sexuality are only two facets of identity that
make up whole humans.

Stigma #4: "You're Brainwashing Kids."
Let's quickly talk about brainwashing. Actual brainwashing
is a nonconsensual process of manipulating a person into
believing something, often by force, and usually happens in
cults. Talking to kids about sexuality and gender isn't brainwashing; it's more like counterprogramming—an antidote
to brainwashing.

We approach nearly everything—history, English, art,
even STEM subjects—through a particular *biased* perspective. In the United States, that perspective is usually that of
white, cisgender, Christian, straight men: the colonizers, the
writers of our history, the perspective through which we
learn about pretty much everything. But this bias is rarely
addressed in formalized educational settings. If you're at all
familiar with anti-racism, all of this might ring a bell.

Anti-racism actively works to undo that bias and re-center
to a BIPOC perspective of these subjects. Methodologies—
like anti-racism—are trying to change the biases that our
current curriculums perpetuate and present new perspectives that widen our lens. What I'm proposing in my work
and the work of this book is that we can continue to widen
our lens by looking at education through a queer and trans
perspective. Our children are already learning within a system that has a very narrow and biased perspective of the
world. The work you are embarking upon critiques our education system and reframes our educational practice to be
more queer-centered.

REFLECTION

Alright! Whew, that was some *heavy* stuff to get through! I'll be honest, it's not always sunshine and daisies from here on out, but I promise the glitter and rainbows are coming! I know that I started all of this by talking about spreading queer joy and these first few sections haven't been all that joyful. That's because I'm not interested in joy for the sake of joy. I'm not interested in a toxic positivity that cracks a forced toothy smile and pretends like everything is alright, because it's not. It is incredibly difficult to be a queer and trans young person in this world because of everything this introduction has laid out, from horrific statistics to childism to internalized anti-queer and anti-trans stigmas particularly around children. So how can we take all of that in while continuing to pursue our mission—to spread queer joy? What I need you to understand about spreading queer joy is that we do not lean into joy to pretend our suffering does not exist. That is (1) not possible, and (2) a disservice to individual and communal queer and trans histories. Instead, we spread queer joy *in spite* of suffering. Our Great Joy is born of our Great Suffering. You cannot spread queer joy without understanding its origin.

KEY TAKEAWAYS

• It is *incredibly difficult* to grow up queer and trans in our society.

• Coupling childism with anti-queer and anti-trans stigmas puts queer, trans, and nonbinary children at great risk.

• You have to work through your conscious and unconscious biases around queerness and kids in order to move forward in this mission.

• We celebrate and spread queer joy in spite of queer suffering, not to hide it.

Part II

INFANCY (AGES 0–1)

LET'S START AT THE VERY BEGINNING

It is *never* too early to start exposing your kids to queer and gender-affirming social justice topics and media. Parents and caregivers might prepare *physically* for a new baby by painting the nursery and buying (or making!) baby clothes. They might prepare *financially* for a new baby by starting a savings fund for their future. And they might prepare *mentally* by perusing *What to Expect When You're Expecting* and the full catalog of baby-prepping books and blogs and podcasts galore. So why can't they also prepare *philosophically* for how they might want their new human to experience the world?

This first phase to rearing children queerly is a vital step of preparation so you're ready for your tiny new human to breach the world. In this chapter, we'll explore ways you can prepare yourself *and* your baby's environment to establish a queer and gender-affirming foundation.

> ## A FEW THINGS TO REMEMBER ABOUT BABIES
>
> • They won't remember anything specific from this time in their lives, so this age is more about you than them.
>
> • Concentrate on the *environment* you create around your infant rather than the details.
>
> • Don't get too caught up in minutia—you're laying the groundwork for the years ahead!

SKIP THE GENDER REVEAL PARTY

Let's get this big-ticket item out of the way first. There is an incredible amount of pressure on new parents to learn about their fetus's genitalia. It is inescapable. Your doctor will ask if you want to know. Then your parents and your spouse's parents and your friends and your friends' friends and your colleagues and your grocer and probably almost everyone you meet will ask if you are having a boy or a girl. It is *the* question we have been programmed to ask pregnant and expecting people. "What are you having?"

So how do you deal with these situations? Here are a few suggestions: If someone asks what you're having, tell them you're having a baby! You can tell them the gender you've decided for them with the caveat that it's only a guess. Or, if you have the energy, explain that your child will tell you their gender when they are older and you don't want to guess for them yet. If you are in an unsafe situation, you can always tell a little white lie and say that you don't know yet. Or come up with your own creative answer. The key here is to disrupt the harmful questioning and weird fascination our society has with immediately sticking new humans into gender boxes. We shouldn't do that to people when they hold active roles in society, let alone before they enter the world! So why not redirect and talk about why you're excited about having a baby, or how cute they'll look in the onesie a loved one gifted you? There are a lot of exciting things about babies that have absolutely nothing to do with their presumed gender.

Here's the thing: No matter what the doctor tells you, you will not know your child's gender until your child is old enough to communicate their gender to you. Until then, you are *guessing* their gender without their consent. You might be right, and that's great! But you also might be wrong, and that's not so great. That's why gender reveal parties are not okay. Not only have they caused catastrophic wildfires, but they are an incredibly harmful tool that reinforces gender roles and stereotypes in our society. Even before a baby is born, they are relegated to boy versus girl, blue versus pink, pants versus dresses, and masculine versus feminine without any say in the matter. Even Jenna Karvunidis, the person credited with first pioneering gender reveal parties has regrets about it—because her child turned out to be queer!

In conclusion, don't throw a gender reveal party and don't attend them. They reinforce gender assignment and celebrate cisness. Just don't do it, please?

WHAT TO SAY WHEN . . . SOMEONE ASKS ABOUT YOUR BABY'S GENDER

Here's an example of one way you can handle questions about your baby's gender.

PERSON

I can't believe you're having a baby! Congratulations!

YOU

Thank you! We're really, *really* excited about it!

PERSON

So! Do you *know* yet?

YOU

Well, we know that the baby is healthy and *kicking*!

PERSON

Oh, I mean do you know if it's going to be a boy or a girl?

YOU

We don't know yet. We're waiting until they're old enough to tell us themselves!

PERSON

Hmmm, but what can I get you for your baby shower, then, if I don't know if it's a boy or a girl?

YOU

You can get the baby anything you like! Books, clothes, infant-safe toys, and newborn supplies are all very much appreciated, thanks for asking!

Sometimes folks will be genuinely curious and sometimes folks will be rude and continue to pry.

Set boundaries for yourself around these conversations and how far you are willing to go with folks. You might even have different answers for different people depending on your comfort level. You might want to practice these responses with a partner or friend, or you can even add a note about how you've decided to approach gender with your child in your social media pregnancy or birth announcement (if that's something you're doing). There are lots of different ways to communicate these decisions; you simply have to find the methodology that comes most naturally to you and your family!

GENDER CONSCIOUS PARENTING

The question still stands: How do I deal with my new human's gender before they tell me what it is? Here is where we'll talk about *gender creative parenting*.

Gender creative parenting is a new term for a parenting philosophy that "promotes gender equality and the freedom to express oneself without stereotypical gender restrictions or expectations," according to Dr. Kyl Myers and their husband, who talk about their journey in their book *Raising Them*. Together, they raised their child, Zoomer, as a nonbinary kid with they/them pronouns.

Gender creative parenting is incredibly new and there is no agreed upon way to do it. With that in mind, I humbly propose an amendment from gender creative parenting to gender *conscious* parenting. The reason behind my thinking is that—and this is something that comes up a lot for trans parents in particular—using they/them pronouns for your child is still assigning them a gender. Nonbinary is a gender. That's not to say that choosing to use they/them pronouns for your child is an inherently *bad* strategy; it's simply that you need to be aware of the fact that you are still assigning your child a gender, before they can tell you themselves.

The tendency here is to overcorrect. Assigning your child they/them pronouns in protest of the gender binary could be akin to not allowing your assigned-female children to play with princesses and wear pink. Some parents want to overcorrect their own childhood by going the opposite way of what society tells them should be in line with their child's gender assignment, when in reality, they're only imposing more or different restrictions. And you already know that if you tell a child they can't have the princess doll or can't wear pink, that's all they're ever going to want.

The emphasis on gender creative parenting has, so far, been mostly about the question "What pronouns should *I* use for my child?" when the question should be "How can I *prepare* my child for the binary-gendered world I am raising them in?" The difference is nuanced, but it's important because gender *conscious* parenting is a lot more complicated than assigning your child they/them pronouns, and can be dependent upon individual families and the kind of labor you are willing to take on.

For example, as Dr. Myers and their husband were raising Zoomer with they/them pronouns, their family presented primarily as a straight- and cis-passing family. Meaning, despite Dr. Myers's queer (and now, nonbinary) identity, they and their husband look like straight, cisgender parents. While they are not actually a straight and cis-gender family, that's how they are most likely perceived by others as they walk through the world. That passing privilege gives them, potentially, a lot more room for the emotional labor involved in parenting a kid with assigned they/them pronouns. Dr. Myers details the constant conversations they had to have with the people in their lives (family members, teachers, school administrators, and other parents) about respecting Zoomer's assigned pronouns in almost every interaction. These constant conversations actively worked to dismantle the gender binary for Zoomer *and* for everyone around Zoomer. That's awesome! It's the kind of work I do almost every day as a nonbinary person living in a binary world, but it's not something that's feasible for every parent, particularly trans parents and queer and trans parents of color.

Compare Dr. Myers's experience raising Zoomer with Trystan Reese's experience raising his kids. Trystan is a trans man in a queer-presenting relationship. Trystan and his husband are already challenging preconceived notions about family as soon as they walk out of the house, first as same-sex parents, second when others learn that Trystan is a trans man, and third when people find out that Trystan carried their son as a trans man. To do the work of also assigning their child they/them pronouns is a lot of added emotional labor for a queer-presenting family like Trystan's. To other families that have multiple marginalized identities, that additional emotional labor and pressure to explain and educate others while navigating microaggressions and keeping their family safe is a lot to hold. It's awesome that Dr. Myers and their husband were able to parent Zoomer in a way that felt comfortable to them and their family's relationship to gender and sexuality, but not every family has the same capacity.

A few years after their book was published, Dr. Myers continued to document Zoomer's gender creative upbringing. As part of their gender creative parenting style, Dr. Myers did pronoun check-in practice with Zoomer. Their practice goes both ways, with four-year-old Zoomer asking Dr. Myers, "Hey, Mom, what pronouns do you want me to use for you today?" And Dr. Myers asked Zoomer for his pronouns that day, too. Around Zoomer's fourth birthday, Dr. Myers asked, "What pronouns are you into for yourself these days, Zoomer?" And Zoomer responded, "I love he/him!" This gender *consciousness* that they've instilled in Zoomer through frequent pronoun check-ins gave him the space and time to declare the pronouns that felt best to him, *when* they felt best to him.

We need to shift our focus from a child's pronouns to actively raising them to be *conscious* of both their own gender feelings *and* the gendered world we live in, through techniques I've outlined. If you want to assign your child they/them pronouns, go ahead! If you want to use pronouns that align with the gender your child was assigned at birth, go ahead! What matters more than your child's assigned pronouns is that you are having active and conscious conversations around gender consistently with them so that when they begin to form their gender identity, they have room to experiment and claim different pronouns from the ones they were assigned. You can (and should) talk to them about their pronouns, but also consider how you (and your child) might assume other people's pronouns and how the way our binary-gendered society puts pressure on our identities and how we perpetuate those binary-gendered ideas onto *others*. And *that* is gender conscious parenting.

INFANCY IS PRACTICE TIME

So, you've made some important philosophical parenting decisions and your brand-new human is finally out of their uterine cocoon and in the world. Congratulations! You made a human. That's awesome and absolutely *wild* that our bodies can do that. So now what? You've successfully dodged questions about your baby's gender, had a ton of fun decorating your gender-neutral nursery, but what do you do *with* the baby?

To start, let's practice building a queer and gender-affirming environment for your child by making sure that you and the people around your baby are not projecting their own assumptions about gender or sexuality onto them. You're going to work on modeling good practices around consent, and you're going to start working on your library of board books and picture books, develop your own literacy around children's media, and think about the conversations you want to have with your child around the media they are exposed to. Let's break it down.

A QUEER AND GENDER-AFFIRMING ENVIRONMENT

We make a lot of assumptions about tiny humans and who they will grow up to be. We've talked about how we (doctors especially) make assumptions about gender, but also about sexuality and other aspects of who kids become—whether they're a boy who will grow up to love football like his dad or a girl who will grow up to love dance like her mom. We make lots of assumptions about who babies will grow up to be and do, and who they will grow up to *love*.

Have you ever seen a blue baby onesie that says "future ladies' man"? That baby onesie—that folks will most likely purchase for babies with penises—immediately assumes that baby will turn out to be straight or heterosexual. But that baby is only a baby. They don't know their sexuality yet and neither does the parent. That baby could grow up to be straight, yes, but they could also grow up to be gay or bisexual or pansexual or anywhere else along the spectrum of human sexuality. We make these heterosexual assumptions like we make cisgender assumptions because we live in a heteronormative and cisnormative world. This is why most queer and trans people have to come out at some point in their lives.

A FEW IDEAS FOR GENDER-NEUTRAL NURSERY ROOM DECOR

Your child's room doesn't have to be gendered to be fun!

• **Outer space:** Dark walls with glow-in-the-dark ceiling stickers forming constellations, a planet mobile above the crib, and an androgynous astronaut!

• **Ocean:** A stuffed octopus for cuddling, a beach mural on the wall, and maybe even a pet goldfish or betta fish if you're ambitious!

• **The sky:** Painted clouds on the ceiling! The sun with a huge smile and cool shades, and a rainbow blankie for swaddling.

Coming out is as much about a queer and/or trans person's personal journey of self-discovery as it is about having to disrupt these assumptions we make about them in infancy. Personally, I despise coming out. I find it awkward and emotional and, honestly, kind of invasive. Coming out is rarely a *fun* experience. For many, me included, it's riddled with anxiety. I have to go into any kind of "coming out" interaction knowing that I'm correcting someone's assumption about me because they have come to their own conclusions about who I am without consulting me first. And queer and trans people can't always know if someone will take well to having their assumptions disrupted, especially if that person is in a position of privilege or power.

So, putting your assigned-male infant in a blue onesie that says "future ladies' man" might seem cute in the moment, but is harmful and could negatively impact your child's future and mental health.

BABY CLOTHES

So, what kinds of baby clothes should you put on your infant? It's easier than you think. You can get tons of gender-neutral onesies, but you don't have to stick with those. As long as you avoid "future ladies' man" onesies and others that perpetuate harmful gender and sexuality assumptions, the rest of the infancy clothing industry is yours to explore! You have even *more* baby clothes to choose from than you might think. Why not put your assigned-male baby in a dress? Why not put your assigned-female baby in cute little overalls and a cap? Were you bummed to learn that your baby has a penis because you wanted to dress them up in frilly dresses and bows? Well, what's stopping you? What if your assigned-male infant grows up to love dresses and maybe even turns out to identify as a trans woman? They will thank

you for taking baby pictures of them in frilly dresses
that align with their true gender identity. That is an
incredible gift you can give your child. So why not
have a little fun and get *playful* with clothes for your
baby?

BABIES AND CONSENT

Let's talk bodies and babies. When we get to toddlerhood,
we can start having explicit conversations about sharing and
consent and different body parts and so much more, but a
healthy understanding around bodies can start even earlier. I spoke with sex and health educator Justine Ang Fonte
about the ways we can introduce age-relevant conversations
around our bodies to children. The phrase she repeated over
and over was, "Womb to tomb!" It starts at the start.

So, let's look at one way we can address topics like consent and our bodies practically from infancy, starting with
how we change a baby's diaper. I promise we are not going to be asking babies if we can change their diaper or not.
You're not asking an infant *if* you can change their diaper,
because there are obviously certain decisions we have to
make in order to take care of our infants' little bodies while
they can't exactly take care of themselves yet. Waiting
to change a baby's diaper can cause irritation, discomfort,
and diaper rash, and that's not treating a baby's body kindly
(we'll talk more about the importance of *body kindness* later!).
When children do not yet have communication skills, decisions around their bodies are left in grown-ups' hands, so we
can model what talking about and taking care of our bodies
looks like when changing their diaper.

While we do this, we can practice *modeling* consent and using proper terminology for our bodies by telling infants what we are doing for them. We don't have to explicitly ask for consent when we know we won't get an answer, but we can be transparent about what we are doing and why, so as they grow, they can have a sense of ownership and eventually an understanding of what is happening to their body and why. And we can also use correct body language to describe what we are doing as we change their diaper to teach them core concepts around sex and health education before they can crawl.

DIAPER-CHANGING CONSENT MONOLOGUE

Your diaper-changing monologue might sound a little like this:

YOU

Okay, time to change your diaper! Let's grab a nice clean one and get this stinky one off of you. Okay, I'm going to take the dirty diaper off now. Let's grab a wipe to get the pee-pee off your penis/vulva. Time for some lotion/powder, this might be a little cold. Let's get this new diaper on you, is that too tight? Alright, go team diaper change!

BOOKS ON BOOKS ON BOOKS

Maybe I'm a little biased as a children's writer and creator myself, but I think that by far one of the best ways to bring important conversations and ideas into your baby's life is to talk about them in relation to existing characters, stories, and images you can put in front of them. So let's talk *books*! You probably already know the benefits of reading to your baby—even in utero—but you also have to be conscious of what books you are reading by diversifying your children's library. You can watch and listen to the growing selection of children's media that includes LGBTQ+ characters, and you can be sure to include LGBTQ+-themed books *written by trans and queer authors*. Paying attention to queer authorship is equally as important as the characters and stories themselves.

You probably have a pile of picture books at home, or maybe you do a weekly trip to the library to cycle through different books, or perhaps you've been working on your classroom collection. Maybe you're only starting and aren't sure what to look for yet. No matter where your kid's library lives, it needs to include books with queer characters written by queer authors, and they should look at queerness through all different angles. Vivek Shraya's *The Boy & the Bindi* is a story of transgender expression through an Indian perspective. *When Aidan Became a Brother* by Kyle Lukoff is written by a white trans man and illustrated by Kaylani Juanita, a Black woman, and tells the story of a young Black trans boy. *They Call Me Mix* by Lourdes Rivas and illustrated by Breena Nuñez is about a nonbinary Chicanx teacher and is in both Spanish and English. Your bookshelf should work to depict the full width and breadth of the LGBTQ+ community and beyond. Make sure to prioritize books with queer characters that are written by queer authors and try to buy them from queer or BIPOC-owned independent bookstores!

Having these representations in your home or school or learning environment is absolutely essential and the bare minimum. This practice is the very beginning of how you can queer a child's environment. Your bookshelves and media intake should be as diverse as the world around us. You need LGBTQ+ books; you need books by Black and Brown and Indigenous and Asian and Latine and disabled authors; you need books from authors whose diverse intersections of experience give them different perspectives. This is all a part of building a queer and gender-affirming environment and constructing your spaces to de-center white straight cis narratives, even in infancy.

REFLECTION

Maybe this felt super easy, or maybe it felt really difficult to actively think about creating a queer and gender-affirming environment for your infant, but regardless, you should be really proud of yourself. You established core building blocks that will help your child throughout their entire life. That is a *big deal*. While I don't want to diminish the work of the rest of this book, what you've already done in disrupting your assumptions about your child's potential gender and sexuality, practicing consent and body talk, and building your library are some of the most important things you can do for your baby. So, now what? Let's talk toddlers!

KEY TAKEAWAYS

• Think about infancy as *practice time* for the years and conversations ahead.

• Make an informed and *conscious* decision about how you would like to approach your child's gender with them *and* with others.

- Practice modeling consent with your infant, even if it feels silly.

- Start your picture book collection ASAP.

Part III

TODDLERS (AGES 1–2)

TINY HUMAN SPONGES

Alright, we're out of infancy and now you have a babbling, mostly upright two- to three-foot-tall chaos demon roaming around your house. Godspeed, my friend. We're not quite at the bread and butter of our work yet—that comes with the preschoolers—but we're at least toasting our bread and getting it warm and golden so the butter spreads nice and easy when we get there. We'll start with some broad topics like toddler-friendly queer theory and dig further into age-relevant sex and health education. We're moving from practicing these ideas ourselves and building our environment to implementing these ideas and communicating them to the tiny ones. That way, when they are a little further along, the more specific conversations and vocabulary will be easy peasy lemon squeezy. Let's get started!

**A FEW THINGS TO REMEMBER ABOUT
TODDLERS**

• Toddlers soak up *every little thing*, so be purposeful about what messages they're receiving.

• Don't get caught up in specifics—their brains can't retain or process that kind of information yet. Instead, focus on big overarching concepts and universal truths.

• Always follow their curiosity! They're exploring the world around them, and it's your job to guide them along the way.

QUEER THEORY FOR KIDS

To lay the foundation, let's tackle the idea of queerness. You don't have to *approach* this first with toddlers—like I said before, kids are naturally curious and bring up the topics they want to talk about in their own order by asking questions—but you have to *understand* it first. This is less of a lesson and more of an underlying pedagogy, or the mode by which we are approaching future ideas and concepts. Queerness is the heart of this work, and if you aren't there yet conceptually, the rest of the knowledge you'll (hopefully) gain in these chapters will be rooted in unstable ground. That's because you cannot do the work to center queerness when you don't know what it is or how to effectively communicate it to small children.

QUEER MEANS DIFFERENT

I've talked about queerness *a lot* already, but let's pause for a moment and define it for our kids' purposes. In a nutshell, queer means different. The word I'm using—"different"—is doing a *lot* of work, and we'll tease out some of those complexities soon, but when communicating what queerness is to kids, we can talk about queerness as *difference*.

ACTIVITY: FROOT LOOPS ARE QUEER CHEERIOS

Difference is a concept kids can grasp. You can teach the basic concept of difference to even a toddler. Line up a row of Cheerios and ask your toddler what they see, which will be a row of Cheerios that all look mostly identical to each other. Maybe you'll count them or talk about their shape or color. You know, normal things you'd teach a toddler. But what if you add a Froot Loop to your row of Cheerios. What is *different* about that Froot Loop versus the Cheerio? Again, you can count the Froot Loop and Cheerios, you can talk about the *differences* in color and size and shape. Voilà! Now your toddler knows how to recognize when one thing in a group is different from the rest. It was that easy—and delicious! What's important to emphasize here is that we aren't attaching any negative connotations around differences. A Froot Loop being *different* from a Cheerio doesn't necessarily make it any better or worse, just different.

Here's when you can turn to your handy-dandy picture book collection that you've been working on (right?). There are *tons* of picture books about difference. So, before you make the leap from "Froot Loops are different from Cheerios" to "Froot Loops are queer," you can use your nightly story-time ritual to talk about stories that emphasize difference. A favorite of mine is *Red: A Crayon's Story* by Michael Hall that he originally wrote about his dyslexia.[12] *The Rainbow Fish* by Marcus Pfister is a fantastic example of a story about difference, too. That way you can talk about ways *people* and *characters* can be different, the ways they might be different, and how being different might make someone feel.

Once that's solid and comfy and you have a shared vocabulary and understanding around difference with your child, *then* we can layer on an understanding of queerness rooted in Sedgwick's oppositional, political, and cultural definition that I introduced way back in the beginning of this book. Here, *queer means different* simplifies Sedgwick's theoretical idea of queerness where *difference* is about the ways *queerness opposes* what our heterocentric culture deems "normal." Being queer isn't about being "other than." It's about being in contrast with normality. We're not telling kids that queer people are different *from them,* we're teaching them that queerness is in opposition to what *society* tells us we should be. The difference here is nuanced but crucial because kids need to understand that queer people are not separate from them, rather that queerness is part of their potentiality. Queerness isn't just an existing reality; it's one *possibility* among many.

_____

12 https://www.michaelhallstudio.com/books/bk_red.html.

Maybe you were introduced to the word "queer" as a slur or derogatory term. While the word "queer" does have a history as a derogatory slur, particularly for earlier generations, the term has, by and large, been reclaimed by swaths of the LGBTQ+ community. That being said, some folks— older LGBTQ+ folks, for example—do not feel comfortable using it. That's okay! We all have different experiences with language, and while language shifts over time, not everyone is always on board with that change. Their experience is valid, too.

The word "queer" was originally used as an in-community term—as opposed to an external derogatory term—as early as 1914.[13] It later became co-opted as a slur but was reclaimed in the late 1980s when members of the LGBT community—particularly HIV/AIDS activist groups— began to self-identify as queer. These queer folks *reclaimed* a word that was once weaponized against them to signify their belonging to a larger community of people who felt ostracized by heterocisnormative culture[14]—aka straight and cisgender people, folks who are not a part of the LGBTQ+ community. What was once a vocabulary of oppression has become a community-building tool of revolution. There is now a robust lexicon of academic study and philosophical ideology revolving around this word: queer. The same argument could be said for the term "gay," which was mostly a derogatory slur when I was growing up, but has always

13 https://www.cjr.org/language_corner/queer.php.

14 https://www.npr.org/sections/publiceditor/2019/08/21/752330316/a-former-slur-is-reclaimed-and-listeners-have-mixed-feelings.

been an accepted term in the LGBTQ+ community because it was *our word* first. There is a beautiful and robust history of linguistic reclamation across many communities of marginalized people.[15]

QUICK HISTORY: GAY MEANS HAPPY

According to the Online Etymology Dictionary, the origin of the word "gay" dates back to the twelfth century and came from the Old French word "gai," which meant "joyful, happy; pleasant, agreeably charming; forward, pert; light-colored."[16] It didn't start to refer to sexuality until the 1600s when it began to signify promiscuity—for example a "gay house" was a brothel—and was used as a slur. It continued to be used in this way through the late 1800s.

It only resurfaced as a slang term for "homosexual" in the 1940s, although many believe it was being used underground as an in-community term starting in the early 1900s. It wasn't until the 1960s that "gay" was fully reclaimed by the gay liberation movement in the fight for equal rights after the Stonewall riots.

WATCH: *Origin of Everything*'s video "History of the Word 'Gay.'"[17]

---

15 https://www.in-mind.org/article/from-derogation-to-reclamation-how-does-language-change.

16 https://www.etymonline.com/word/gay.

17 https://www.pbs.org/video/history-of-the-word-gay-bcbiuu/.

So how do we help kids make the leap from understanding difference to *queer means different*? You simply say it! You've already done the hard part by explaining the larger concept of difference. This concept is present and ubiquitous. And we can easily attach the idea of queerness to this feeling of difference, because queerness, after all, is just one *kind* of difference among many. All you need to do is use your newfound knowledge to dig as deep into it as your child wants to go.

BEING DIFFERENT IS AWESOME

What's more important than instilling the lesson that *queer means different* is showing kids that being different—any kind of different, not only queer—is *awesome*! Fred Rogers's mantra was that every child is special. My work builds upon his by framing difference as a kind of specialness: that queer means different, *and* being different is awesome. It's what makes you your wonderful, beautiful self. Maybe that's a queer kid, maybe that's a kid from a queer family, maybe that's a kid who doesn't see themselves in their picture books or TV shows or movies. There is so much sadness and struggle and negativity that surrounds queer identity. It can be incredibly difficult to live as a queer person in this world. There is loss and heartache and oppression and trauma. We must acknowledge these hardships; not doing so would be a disservice to the resiliency of our queer ancestry. But if we are looking toward a queer future, wouldn't we want to push forward queer joy and queer happiness and queer hope?

Your job is to actively speak to those kids and validate their otherness, turning it from something negative and lonesome into an identity with community—that includes lots of awesome people—affirming their difference as a positive asset, and a source of courage and strength in itself.

This way of talking about queerness empowers queer and trans youth while *also* inspiring allies. Because we are all different and queerness is a kind of difference, we're not really that different from each other, right? And if everyone is different, then we have a collective understanding of what it means and feels like to *be different* in one way or another. Our differences become something we all have in common. While a cisgender kid with straight parents might not understand what it means to have two moms or to be a trans kid, they can still *empathize* with that kid because they recently moved and they're the new kid at school, and they understand what it means to be different through their own lens. They understand that it can be hard and scary and lonely and exciting all at the same time; that is powerful allyship.

If we teach kids early on that's it's okay—even *awesome*—to be different, there would be a lot less bullying in schools and a lot less bigotry in the world at large, because we are teaching young people to practice empathy, and become open to listening to others' struggles that are different from our own. Empathy is a muscle we must stretch and flex and work at; it's not something that comes without nurture. Childhood is the primary training ground for empathy. And there's neuroscience research to back that up! Exposure to stories, characters, and experiences that teach us what it's like in someone else's shoes help kids build a capacity for imagination that includes experiences outside of their own.

Humanity is multitudinous and complex, and most people do not fit into nice neat little identity boxes. We are all different and our differences are not the same, but all of those differences are awesome, no matter what they are, and the ability to build our empathy muscle with that understanding is what gets us to a better world. And there are lots of fantastic ways to help your kid build empathy for queer folks!

WHAT TO DO WHEN . . . SOMEONE USES "QUEER" AS A DEROGATORY WORD

This is point-blank not okay. The same goes for using the word "gay" as a slur. There are other words that also shouldn't be used, but I won't be listing them here, because they do not deserve the space. If you hear someone using a derogatory term against the LGBTQ+ community, you should call them out for it, even if it means calling out a student in front of their class. This is important to do because you are demonstrating to the other kids in the space that it is not okay to use words like "gay" or "queer" or anything akin in a hurtful way.

If you're talking to a young person, consider having a discussion with them about their use of the word and correcting their definition, because that's the issue here: they're using these words incorrectly. If a child calls someone "gay" to be hurtful, we might call it out in the moment and sit them down individually to ask them what they think that word means. Then, we can deal with the word's incorrect usage, separate from the potential bullying or violence of the situation (which might indicate other underlying problems that child is facing). These instances need to be dealt with. When they are left alone, that person will continue to use these words incorrectly and in a harmful way.

AGE-RELEVANT SEX ED IS ABUSE PREVENTION

Before we dive into this next section, I want to pause. If all of this is relatively new to you, if your brain is in a bit of a tailspin right now, that's okay. If not, that's great, you're doing awesome. If yes, that's still great! You're still doing awesome. Please be patient with yourself. We are rebuilding your way of looking at the world, and working on how you can communicate that to young people, and that process can take time.

Here is where we get into a little bit of sex ed. We'll get to "The Talk" and how to make it more queer-inclusive eventually, but that's not the conversation I'm most interested in here. We are still talking about toddlers after all!

As we've established, folks are incredibly sensitive about kids and sexuality. We've addressed this discomfort when it comes to queerness, but when it comes to sex and health education, people aren't always sure how to handle it. I know I didn't at first. I've pushed the boundaries of what's "acceptable" and "appropriate" plenty. I did, after all, name my preschool web series *Queer Kid Stuff.* While the in-yer-faceness of the title has helped earn the series acclaim, it's also brought its own repercussions. Repercussions like mobs of angry internet trolls, one unsubstantiated death threat, and an ongoing lawsuit with a media behemoth. Repercussions that make sex and health education for the preschool sect almost taboo even for *me* to touch.

I was incredibly nervous to make sex ed–related episodes of *Queer Kid Stuff*. It was different territory for me. While I do think my work is completely "appropriate" and age-relevant, I was scared of intensified scrutiny. I was scared of the stigmas already attached to queer work for kids. That someone might actually report me as a sex offender and turn it into a legal battle, potentially causing me to lose my full-time job at a pre-school and after-school program, and putting a future career in this work in jeopardy. The benefit of going whole hog on these ideas at the time did not, for me, outweigh the cost. And I wasn't totally off base! But! I think we are in a different place now. I think the conversations have moved far enough forward and have matured in a way where we can push the envelope.

Even if you're open to it, the idea that sex ed topics are age-relevant for toddlers and preschoolers might be completely new to you. However, avoiding these ideas is actively harmful to young children, so we're going to go through it all step-by-step, like we did in the previous chapters.

To reiterate: Talking about sex and health education with infants, toddlers, and preschoolers doesn't mean we are talking about intercourse. There is a way to approach sex education that is developmentally "appropriate" and, more importantly, *relevant* for young children, and the questions they might be having at their prepubescent age.

Queer Kid Stuff did a short sex ed series, which included episodes about why we shouldn't ask people about their bodies; an episode focused on body positivity, challenging children to create their own positive affirmations for themselves; and a reading of Cory Silverberg's fantastic picture book *What Makes a Baby*, which elegantly and honestly explains where babies come from, in a trans- and nonbinary-inclusive way. These ideas are stepping stones to larger topics that fall under sex education, bringing this curriculum down to the early childhood sect.

Practicing relevant sex and health education from "womb to tomb" is not only important for your child's general well-being, but it's also about their physical safety. The way our society treats and addresses sex and health education is incredibly oppressive, actively making young people vulnerable to trauma and sexual assault. We worry so much about protecting young children from harm, but often grown-ups make the grave mistake of trying to step in on behalf of children, instead of providing them with tools they could use to protect *themselves*. That is what age-relevant sex and health education can accomplish. That doesn't mean that kids don't need adult help and support in unsafe situations—they absolutely do. But we can give them the tools to be advocates for their own bodies.

In our conversation, sex educator Justine Ang Fonte told me, "Because we live in a world that does not prioritize children's body agency, it means that we have enabled people in our population to take advantage of the most vulnerable, which are our children." If you are interested in giving the young folks in your life important information that will directly affect their safety and the safety of others, come into this section with an open mind because age-relevant sex and health education *is abuse prevention*.

When I spoke with Fonte further, she articulated the three core principles we must impart to young children:

1) We can teach them *body kindness*—to love and be kind to their bodies so they can care for themselves,

2) we can teach them *body ownership*—the idea that

they, and no one else, are in control of their bodies, and the role consent plays, and

3) we can teach them *body language*—the language
we use for our bodies, so we can communicate
our body's needs clearly and with accurate vocabulary.

These are powerful tools of abuse prevention, because
when a child knows that they have control over their own
body, they can recognize when they are being violated or
harmed; and when someone is unkind and uncaring of their
body, they can recognize and counteract that unkindness;
and when something happens to their body, they have the
language to communicate it properly. These are the tools
that keep young children safe.

In giving children an understanding of consent, and promoting ideas like body kindness and ownership, we are giving them tools with which they can protect (and celebrate!)
themselves and their bodies, and in parallel, build an underlying respect for other people's bodies as well. Doing this
in the toddler years is *especially* important because we are
trying to instill these ideas before they are able to absorb
and internalize any negative ideas around bodies like anti-
fatness, ableism, and colorism, to name a few. When we address ideas around body kindness, ownership and consent,
and language with kids as young as two and three, we can
get to them first, before the magazines full of skinny white
models tell them all the ways their body doesn't conform
to Western beauty standards. This is especially important
for kids who are Black or Brown or Asian or Latine or disabled or trans or fat or anything else society doesn't chris-
ten as "conventionally attractive." This work in particular

preserves a child's body *neutrality* and self-kindness as long as humanly possible.

BODY KINDNESS

Let's start with *body kindness*. Body kindness goes beyond body positivity and self-care, and into the territory of radical self-love found in Sonya Renee Taylor's book *The Body Is Not an Apology*. Body kindness says that our bodies deserve respect from ourselves *and* from others. There are three things we need to understand and display to children:

1. Think about your body with kindness.

When was the last time you were kind to your body? Maybe you did a face mask last Sunday or had a glass of wine in the tub. Or maybe it was last month? Or last year?! When was the last time you took twenty minutes out of your day to soothe your body and thank it for all it does for you? How can you model a body kindness practice for your child? How can you include them in your practice *and* help them develop a practice of their own?

Understanding body kindness seems simple, but it's probably the hardest principle for adults. Like we've grown up in a heterocisnormative world, we've been inundated with unreachable ideals of Western beauty since infancy. Bodies that our society deems "good" are typically gender-conforming: thin, light-skinned, have smooth skin and hair, and are able-bodied. The message is: I must fix my body to be good and worthy and valuable. But most people simply don't look like that!

We grown-ups—me included!—need to do away with the idea of good and bad, worthy and unworthy, valuable and useless bodies. All bodies are good. All bodies are worthy. All bodies are valuable. All bodies are human. All bodies are our own and no one else's to control. We have to actively combat messages from mainstream media by diversifying the types of bodies that are depicted around us, making sure we are seeing examples of folks who are dark-skinned, or with natural textured hair, or with gender nonconforming expressions, or with acne or a physical disability or fat! There are so many different ways for our bodies to look and *every body is beautiful*. We can undo the faults of the images that raised us to apply value to our bodies by letting kids know that their bodies are perfect the way they are, no matter their size or shape or skin tone or hair texture or ability.

So next time you look in the mirror, and negative body talk rears its head, pause for a moment to reframe your thoughts toward *kindness* toward yourself and your body. Try imagining a friend talking to you the way you talk to yourself. Would you stand for it if your friend said, "Wow, you look horrible today"? Or if someone spoke to your child that way? Absolutely not! This isn't always easy to do, especially for grown-ups who struggle with eating disorders, body dysphoria/dysmorphia, and other body image issues. That's something to figure out and work through. But even if you can't always be kind to your body, let's show kids how they can. How can you model your own learning and shift toward kindness for the kids in your life?

2. Feed your body kindness.
Fonte describes *feeding* your body with kindness, "not just with your mouth, but [with] things, your eyes, your being, the things your ears are being fed, the things your skin is

touching and being fed." Feed your body and your *soul* with kindness through every mode of input: By reading kind books, listening to kind people and music, and bringing joy to your body—and choosing to keep out those things that tell you that you and your body aren't enough. And, of course, literally feeding yourself kindly, with food that nourishes your body and provides energy and makes you *feel good*. That doesn't mean eat "clean" or "healthy," or latch on to whatever diet fad is currently trending. It means we are giving our bodies food that nourishes our bodies in *many* ways! How can you show the kids in your life how you nourish your body and help them understand how they can feed *their* bodies? It could be as simple as splashing around in a bubble bath with them, or having an impromptu dance party before bed, or following the trend of TikTok parents teaching their toddlers to cook for themselves. The sky's the limit!

3. Believe that you deserve kindness.

Finally, we have to ensure that we are treated kindly by others, and affirm that we and our bodies are deserving of kindness. Fonte told me, "[these ideas] sound very simple, but even for adults, [they're] a radical belief that we don't have, because of a lot of different oppressions that have told us otherwise. But if we can affirm that our bodies are deserving of kindness, and other's bodies are deserving of kindness, we might live in a more safe, fulfilling, and pleasurable world." The same principles we teach them should also be applied to ourselves. If we're telling kids they deserve kindness, one of the best things we can do for them is to model it ourselves! So how are you showing them that you deserve kindness, too?

ACTIVITY: WRITE YOUR OWN AFFIRMATIONS

A fantastic way to put all of this into action is through *affirmations*. Affirmations—a sentence or set of sentences that you can repeat aloud or to yourself for a positive boost—are a great way to physically practice body kindness. You can even work them into a morning ritual at home or in the classroom. So grab your kid and a mirror, and repeat these words together:

"I am strong! I am brave! I am beautiful! I am awesome! I am me!"

This is a starting point; you can make up your own affirmation that works for you and the young folks you're with. One of my personal favorite affirmations comes from queer astrologer Chani Nicholas: "May I be bolstered by the confidence the universe has in me." Affirmations are powerful things! Creating and practicing your own affirmation is one way to develop a body kindness practice with your toddler.

BODY OWNERSHIP AND CONSENT

I own my body, you own your body, your kid owns their body; it's that plain and simple. It doesn't matter your age, it doesn't matter whether you're Black or white or Brown or Asian or Latine or disabled or cis or trans, *you—and only you—own your body*. You've already planted the seeds of consent with your infants, so let's take those practices into toddlerhood.

As they grow, children develop an understanding that

their bodies are their own. Beyond our language around diaper changing and consent, toddlers can start to make *some* decisions about their bodies. They can choose what they do or do not want for their body, of their own volition and no one else's. This idea is pivotal to a child's safety. It's not only about knowing that they can say yes or no, it's about understanding that they have the ability to control who touches their bodies, when, how, and where. When a child understands consent and ownership of their body, they understand when they can say no to someone when they might be under pressure, particularly from a grown-up.

CONSENT AND HUGGING

A great way to model consent is with hugging. Not every child wants to be hugged and squeezed all the time like an adult might think! It's great practice in modeling consent to ask your child—no matter how old they are—if it's okay to hug them. I know what you're thinking: *They're my child and I should be able to hug my child without asking them!* But here's the thing— the goal behind this practice isn't really about the hug. It's about teaching body ownership. If a child is taught that they own their body and are the only person who can give consent to others to be in their space and do things—anything—to their body, then they will understand when someone is crossing their personal bodily boundaries without their permission. So, if they say no to a hug, see if they want a high five instead! And if they don't want that, either, don't take it personally. The lesson is more important.

The first sex ed *Queer Kid Stuff* video I made was all about consent. At the time, *The New York Times*' Jodi Kantor and Megan Twohey and *The New Yorker*'s Ronan Farrow had exposed Harvey Weinstein as a rapist and sexual predator at the height of the #MeToo era. I wanted to talk to kids about this important moment in a way that made sense to them and felt relevant to their lives. I decided to tackle the idea of consent through a new song, which drove home the lesson that yes means yes and no means no and that we have to respect other people's boundaries. Words and phrases like "maybe," "perhaps tomorrow," "not now," and "how about later?" are not explicit yeses, and therefore they mean no.

This is what we're talking about when we speak about consent. Consent is all about permission! It doesn't matter if we're talking about our bodies, our toys, our time: it all boils down to consent and giving someone permission to touch our bodies, to use our toys, and to take up our time. You, and only you, have control and the ability to give permission for these things that are yours, and the same goes for young children, even toddlers! They are the only ones who have full and complete ownership over their bodies and can give *permission* or consent for someone to touch their bodies.

CONSENT AND SHARING

You can also teach consent by practicing sharing. This is something that probably pops up a *lot* during everyday play with friends, siblings, and family members. Sharing is a great way to get into conversations around consent because it's all about permission! We're not only learning that we have ownership of our own bodies, we are learning that *others* have ownership of their bodies. Toddlers need to learn how to give permission when it's asked of them and why. Let's say your toddler is on a playdate and another child really wants to play with your toddler's favorite toy. Here is a perfect opportunity to explain to them that giving the other child *permission* and *consent* to play with their toy will make that other child happy, exactly how they feel when they play with it. They're not only learning how to give permission and consent, but why they might give their permission or consent to someone and how that can be a good and fun thing. We're continuing to build up their empathy muscle and understand others' feelings and experiences outside of their own!

If consent isn't being practiced or taught to kids, then boundaries around permission are going to be blurred because they won't have a solidified concept of their ownership of their body. Down the line, this can lead directly to situations where children are vulnerable to predatory adults. A child who does not understand that they own their body and have the ability to choose to tell someone yes or no is less likely to enforce a boundary with an adult who is touching them inappropriately. A child who does understand that they own their own body is more likely to recognize when they have not given permission and someone is violating their body ownership. We can teach them specifically about the parts of their bodies that are private; that, in Fonte's words, "if there is another person that is ever touching [your privates] or seeing [your privates], it's because you as a child have made that decision . . . and [have] the ability to change your mind about that too." When we give children tools and help them understand body ownership and how to use consent as a tool of that ownership, they can protect themselves—and respect other people's bodies, too.

Now, these consent practices won't always be perfect. Childhood and parenting are messy and chaotic and sometimes you have to strap them into the car seat—as they kick and scream—to go to Grandma's house so you don't miss your flight for a business trip. What's important to understand in these moments is that there's probably a reason your child is kicking and screaming. Maybe the strap is too tight and doesn't fit their body correctly. Maybe they're tired and are still learning how to regulate their emotions when they are sleepy—I mean, I'm a grown-up and I'm still not great at that, ask my wife! We can't always turn every hard moment into a learning opportunity and that's okay. But we can try to breathe through the moment with them and teach them to communicate what is going on in their body. What exactly is wrong with the car seat? "Are you hungry? Are you tired? Can you use your words to tell me what is going on in your body?"

These conversations and active communications that happen between you and your child show that you respect them and their bodies and can give them a "why" for what is happening. You might not get their explicit permission or consent in these moments, but at least you communicated your reasoning. Because even for adults, there are times when the safety of our bodies trumps our comfort. We can teach toddlers that we sometimes have to do things we don't want to for our own safety and in order to respect other people's needs. Giving permission can be about taking care of others as much as it is about taking care of ourselves.

The child who understands consent and bodily autonomy is also more likely to talk to an adult they trust about a sexually inappropriate situation. Through these conversations, they should understand that they alone can make important decisions about their bodies, particularly about the ways grown-ups touch them. With that context and practice, they can recognize when someone violates their consent. They can then communicate what happened to them. So many kids feel like they have to keep a grown-up's "secret" of assaulting them because they are ashamed, they think they are the ones who did something wrong. Teaching them consent as a toddler shows them that what is *really* shameful is someone else violating their consent. So, while asking permission to hug your child might feel awkward and weird and silly, it's about so much more than a hug.

Maybe you're noticing a pattern: teaching these things not only validates these ideas for the young person you're directly talking to but also greatly benefits the young folks around that child and how your child treats others throughout their life. In conversations about gender, sexuality, and identity, kids feel valid in experimenting with and exploring and stating their own identities, while also supporting and building empathy and *allyship* for those around them. The same goes for consent. All of this work is ultimately about spreading queer joy, yes, but on a larger scale, making the world a kinder place for everyone no matter who they are or what their background is.

BODY LANGUAGE

The sex and health education episodes of *Queer Kid Stuff* use anatomically correct language. At the time I was nervous about how folks would react to sex education videos aimed at a preschool audience, and I wanted to make sure that parents and educators were prepared to hear me talk about penises and vaginas and vulvas in the videos. I wish I didn't have to put that disclaimer on there, because I wish that grown-ups would stop being scared of using correct body language around kids, even and especially toddlers. "Penis," "vagina," and other words we use for our bodies are not bad or scary words—they're terms we should be able to learn and use the same way we learn about our "elbows" or our "cheeks." They are simply other parts of our bodies. The only difference is that these parts of our bodies are private, because they are vulnerable and need to be protected. Using euphemisms for these body parts and shying away from direct language insinuates that we should feel shame. If you model shame around the word, you also model shame around what the word symbolizes. If a child learns and feels that, then they will probably also feel shame if something happens to that body part.

Think for a moment about why you might be hesitant to use correct body language with the kids in your life. Is it because you are uncomfortable using those words? If so, think about why. Were you raised that way? Why do you think you were taught to feel uncomfortable with body words or body parts, for that matter? Do you want to continue that cycle? How might your life be different if you had been raised to ask questions and use direct language around your body parts? We not only need to talk about our bodies with anatomically correct language, but we also need to know how to use that language in an inclusive way.

First: there is no such thing as a "boy body" or a "girl body." This is incredibly important to reinforce with children if they are going to understand transgender (and intersex!) identities when we get to them! A boy with a vagina is a boy, and a girl with a penis is a girl, point-blank. While we are assigned our gender at birth because of our genitalia, genitalia itself is another body part; it doesn't inherently have a gender any more than our arms have a gender.

This might be a big, new idea, so take a moment to pause and reflect. Remember what you learned in the preceding chapter about gender and gendered language. Stripping gendered language from body parts is easy if we use correct body language with toddlers. Make sure that when you use correct body language, you're not associating that body language with any particular gender. Talk about penises like you might talk about elbows. Elbows don't have gender like penises don't have gender. Some people have penises and some people don't. If you're thinking, "Well, everyone has elbows, that's not the same as penises," have you thought about how some disabled people might not have elbows? This is a little bit beside the point, but start thinking about how you can be more inclusive in your language around bodies that might be unexpected and how bodies and the parts that make up our bodies are not ubiquitous to any one experience, especially any one person's experience of their gender.

But sometimes, even toddlers might already associate genitalia with gender. So how do we undo that with our kids? Using toys is an easy example. Barbies are typically in the girl toy aisle and superheroes are typically in the boy toy aisle. Now what if a boy wants a Barbie—is that Barbie still a "girl's toy"? Same for the superheroes: if a girl picks up a superhero toy, is it still a "boy's toy"? The girl-ness or boy-ness of a toy doesn't have to do with the toy itself, but with the ownership of the toy. If a girl has a penis, her penis isn't a boy's penis, it's that girl's penis. And if a boy has a vulva, then his vulva isn't a girl's vulva, it's that boy's vulva. Body parts are body parts; what matters is who claims them as their own and how they identify.

BODY LANGUAGE AND BATH TIME

Bath time is the *perfect* time to practice using correct anatomical body language with your child! Like we did with infants, you can describe what you are doing as you do it.

YOU

Alright, let's get some suds on this washcloth so we can get you clean! First, let's wash your face. Close your eyes and mouth so the soap can't get in. Okay, let's scrub your back. Now your chest and belly. Now your arms! Let's start at the top with your upper arms, then your elbow, then your forearms, and in between your fingers. And don't forget your under-arms. Legs next—over your knees and down to your feet and between those toes! Let's wash your vulva/penis. Do you want me to wash it for you or do you want to do it yourself? Make sure your vulva/penis is nice and clean! Alright, let's wash all that soap off your body. Nice job, kiddo!

There you go. Now your kid is squeaky clean *and* they have an introductory anatomy lesson that normalizes language for genitalia.

WHERE DO BABIES COME FROM?

This is the section you might be anticipating the most: How do I answer my *toddler* when they ask me where they came from? How do I talk to toddlers about sex? How do I have "The Talk"? How do I talk about *gay sex*?

If your toddler is asking you the question every parent dreads, "Where do babies come from?" they're most likely *not* asking about sex. They are asking about conception, not about the actual act of sex. Fonte emphasizes that parents should get to the bottom of what kids are really asking them by probing their question, because if you start to ramble about "When two grown-ups love each other . . ." they might shrug their shoulders and say they wanted to know what *exactly* makes a baby.

The answer to that question is not sex; that is a heterosexual-centric way of looking at conception. Sex is one way to make a baby, but there are many ways to make a baby! So, the way we accurately answer this question is by addressing the science. What *makes* a baby is a story of the body, not of sexual intercourse, using three vital ingredients: an egg, a sperm, and a uterus, which can belong to anyone of any gender. And that conception can happen through sexual intercourse between a person with a penis and a person with a vagina, or it can happen at a fertility center where a doctor takes a sperm and an egg to create an embryo and implants that embryo into anyone with a uterus (that includes trans masculine people, too!). It's that simple! That is what makes a baby, and that is an age-relevant conversation you can have with kids as young as two about where babies come from, one that is queer-inclusive, uses correct body language, and relies on a specific *scientific* explanation for creation that de-mystifies and piques kids' curiosity. I also *highly* recommend reading Cory Silverberg's fantastic book *What Makes a Baby* with your littles. It does almost all the work for you!

ANSWER THE QUESTION

When you answer a child's question, are you listening to the *specific* question they are asking and answering that? Or are you answering the question you *think* they are asking? When a child asks, "Where do babies come from?," and your grown-up brain immediately jumps to a conversation about sex, then you're not answering the question they've asked. If you wanted to answer that specific question, you'd respond by talking about how a baby grows in a person's uterus. Once the baby has grown for about nine months in the uterus, then the pregnant person gives birth either through their vagina or a surgery called a C-section and the baby enters the world! Toddlers in particular are incredibly literal, so you'll probably only confuse them if you begin a whole conversation about sex. Before you go down the rabbit hole, carefully listen to the specific question your child is asking, and think about how you can best answer as directly as possible.

REFLECTION

You made it! Welcome to the other side of toddlerhood. We've managed to teach queer theory to one- and two-year-olds and worked through some important sex and health education topics. The ideas in this chapter are absolutely crucial to raising your child in a queer and gender-affirming space, but they also might be the scariest for you to tackle, and that's okay. The objective is to raise a generation of kids who understand that being different is *awesome* and can properly label a textbook anatomy chart before kindergarten.

KEY TAKEAWAYS

• Toddlers are tiny human sponges that soak up every little piece of information and internalize that information to develop their sense of self.

• Queerness is a kind of difference and being different is awesome!

• Age-relevant early childhood sex and health education is abuse prevention.

• Use anatomically correct language with your kid.

• Answer your child's specific questions, not the questions you think they're asking.

Part IV

PRE-K (AGE 3)

THE CRUCIAL YEARS

Get the lunch boxes ready because we're sending the littles off to school! You've made it to the heart of this work, the bread and butter. This moment is when the work matters most. It's also probably the hardest, but don't worry, we'll push through together. You're not alone in this.

These are the Crucial Years. This is the time when we can actively facilitate kids' introduction to the world and help them mold themselves with the language and possibility models we provide. That's why three-year-olds are my absolute favorite kids to work with. Infants and one year-olds are mostly curious blobs who are endlessly entertaining but can't do a whole lot more than eat, sleep, and poop. Two-year-olds are less blob and more human, but they haven't quite figured out themselves or the world yet and are predisposed to chaos because of this. Three-year-olds, on the other hand, are at the very beginning of understanding themselves and the world around them. I love seeing three-year-olds discover their personalities. It's fascinating to watch and helps me reorient myself and take a brand-new look at the world around *me*.

Because you've exposed your kids to basic concepts like queerness, consent, and body kindness, they are already growing up in a space that is actively queer and gender-affirming. Now, we're going to get more concrete and specific. We'll dive headfirst into direct conversations around gender and sexuality and lay the groundwork for more complex topics like intersectionality and activism so they're ready for what's to come when they're off to kindergarten.

A FEW THINGS TO REMEMBER ABOUT PRESCHOOLERS

- Three-year-olds really start to develop their sense of self and self-identify. Give them the tools to help them do this—and don't underestimate them!

- Experimentation, exploration, and play are absolutely key at this age. Be there to cheer them on, validate their discoveries, and get a little weird alongside them!

- These years are the bread and butter of this work. Now is the time to kick things into a higher gear! Go for it!

GENDER IDENTITY, EXPRESSION, AND EUPHORIA

Before we get into it, I want to quickly reiterate that my explanation of gender for kids is not the end-all be-all for how to talk to kids about gender. This is simply what has worked for me. There isn't just one right way to talk about gender with kids; there are many different approaches. Just look at resources like Sam Killermann's the Genderbread Person or Maya Gonzalez's *The Gender Wheel*! While there isn't one right way to talk to kids about gender, there are a bunch of wrong ways! I'm here to steer you in the right direction alongside my incredibly wise peers. So, here's how I explain gender—even to preschoolers!

Gender can be broken down into two ideas: *gender identity* and *gender expression*. Gender identity is about how we *feel*; it's an internal sense that stems from our innermost self. That internal gender feeling is not something I can totally explain because it's different for everyone. I feel it in my chest when I'm wearing my favorite clothes, or after I've gotten a new haircut, or when I see a picture of me that I like, or when someone I love uses my correct pronouns. Note that I used "correct" instead of "preferred" pronouns—a person's pronouns are exactly that. They aren't "preferred," implying that there is a choice or an opinion. When someone uses my *correct* pronouns, it gives me a warm and happy feeling that circulates throughout my whole body. That's what we call *gender euphoria*.

Gender euphoria is sort of a hard feeling to describe, but you know it when you see it, or even feel it for yourself! It's how I felt looking at my new chest the first time after my top surgery. It felt right, and with that rightness came unbridled *joy* seeing my body the way I'd imagined it for so many years. It's like the satisfaction you might feel when you fit the final piece in a jigsaw puzzle. Or like putting on your favorite sweater that fits perfectly. Or getting to eat your favorite food at lunch! Gender euphoria can come from lots of different things, but it's easiest to pinpoint when our internal gender identity matches our external gender *expression.*

So, if gender identity is about how we feel about ourselves, then gender expression is how we express that feeling to the world. It's how we externalize our gender, through our clothes, our hair, our interests, and our pronouns, and so many more things. Where gender identity is abstract and *in the feels,* gender expression is a lot more tangible. Gender expression is the part of gender we *see* and enact in our everyday lives. Pronouns are a form of gender expression that sit close to our gender identity, but our gender expression also is so much more than our pronouns. Gender expression is *gender creativity*! It's the clothes we wear, how we style our hair, how we carry ourselves, how we exercise (or don't!), how we play, how we create; it is embedded in everything we do, because it is how we express our innermost selves. When our gender identity aligns with our gender expression, that's when you might experience gender euphoria. *That's* what we're aiming for. We are our best selves and living our fullest truths when we are gender euphoric.

But you probably didn't pop out knowing the kinds of clothes you like to wear. Figuring out how to best express yourself and your gender is a lifelong experiment that young kids are only beginning. It's all about exercising the muscle that tells us how to make decisions around our gender expression and knowing what feels good and fun and empowering. It is *super* important to encourage creativity and experimentation around gender expression with kids, because this is the time to get wild and try out new things! This age is a crucial window for kids to develop their overall sense of self, and gender is an incredibly important focal point for that work that is typically overlooked. Working

actively on this early with young kids and being supportive of their choices and experimentation—no matter how
wacky!—is paramount.

INTERROGATE YOUR OWN GENDER

Take a moment to think—really *think*—about your
gender. Cisgender grown-ups are rarely forced to
grapple with questions around gender in their lives.
Pause for five minutes to remove words like "male"
and "female" from your head; clear some metaphys-
ical brain space and notice what you feel about your
gender. Try to reach beyond the confines of the gender you've been told you are for your entire life. See
if any memories around gender surface for you, like
times when you especially loved how you presented
yourself. When have you felt gender euphoria? Have
you ever felt uncomfortable in your gender? If you've
never thought about your gender like this before, it
might be tough. Don't worry, there's plenty of time
to practice.

We'll get into the different specific conversations we can
have with the young people in our lives to help them understand these nuanced concepts around identity, so don't
worry that these definitions can sometimes be a little too
abstract for the youngest kiddos.

I'll let you in on a little secret: it doesn't matter if they
fully understand gender as a concept. Even though they probably won't understand everything the first time they hear
it, something will latch. That's the seed of knowledge! We

want to plant these seeds whenever and wherever we can in young people's lives. Some won't take, but others might sprout roots and you never know when that sprout will bloom. What matters is that you are introducing these ideas early, which kick-starts a much longer, years longer, ongoing conversation because—fun fact!—the American Academy of Pediatrics has found that most children have a solid understanding of their gender identity by the age of *four.*

If you are struggling with how you want to approach gender with the kids in your life, start with helping them recognize gender euphoria. Kids understand feelings and emotions. They might not be able to regulate them quite yet, but they can definitely feel them! Helping them recognize and name the specific emotions and feelings around gender euphoria will teach them to recognize and later put language to their gender with tools like pronouns and identity labels. Help them pick out their outfit for school and ask them *how* it makes them feel and *why.* Maybe they love their dress with sunflowers on it because the color yellow makes them happy and the dress spins around them when they twirl. Or maybe they love their green corduroy overalls because they can run fast outside and feel all cozy when they're snuggled up on the couch reading a book with you. Whatever their reasons, get them to observe and think about how they express themselves to the world and how that matches up with how they feel inside. They'll be able to find the language to describe their gender in no time!

But in order for them to understand these concepts, it's maybe even more important for *you* to fully understand and embrace these ideas for yourself. You have to fully grasp these ideas first and foremost so you can continue to restructure your environment in a way that centers and affirms all gender identities and queerness in children's spaces—whether that's regularly checking in about your child's pronouns, diversifying the wardrobe and toys that are available to them, or making sure you've got books on your shelves written by queer and trans authors. Laying this kind of foundational and atmospheric groundwork is incredibly important, because you have no idea when the idea might suddenly click for them.

One day, or slowly over time (depending on the child), they'll start to communicate and ask questions, and follow their curiosity down a path that will lead them toward self-identifying, because they already have a road map for what's possible. Most adults, myself included, had to walk this path without a map; what's cool is that you're not only handing the young person in your life a map, you're handing them a GPS with multiple routes, so they can decide for themselves the road that makes them feel their best without having to do most of the uncovering on their own.

When I look at photos of myself as a young child, I see my most gender euphoric self. I see a kid with a big toothy grin who loves to wear T-shirts and overalls and wants to keep their hair short and shaggy. I loved my short hair and always asked for the "boy haircut," but I also hated being called a boy. My parents were mostly supportive of my tomboyishness, but years of getting misgendered led me to get my ears pierced and grow my hair long, because that's what I thought I was supposed to do. I was tired of having zero control over how others perceived my gender, so I stopped making decisions that aligned with my own sense of my gender, and starting making them to please others. I caved into what I thought I *should* do, rather than what I *wanted* to do. Young folks need to be *actively* encouraged to experiment with their gender expression beyond what is typical for their assigned gender, and they need to be supported vehemently in the choices they make around what expression makes them feel euphoric versus dysphoric.

INTRODUCING PRONOUNS

So you've asked yourself hard questions about the concept of gender, as well as your own identity, and started to seed ideas around gender euphoria with the kids in your life. Understanding your feelings around your gender is the first step. The second is figuring out how you want to express it externally, and *then* you can start to figure out how you want to communicate those feelings and expressions through language. Your journey might not necessarily follow that exact order—gender, after all, is a whole heck of a lot messier than that—but following those steps with children helps them at such a young age. Now let's give them the tools to communicate their gender feelings. Let's teach them about *pronouns*.

Pronouns usually—but not always—indicate our gender. You'll remember we've already talked about pronouns in the section on gender creative parenting! Some people use "she" and "her" as their pronouns, some use "he" and "him," some use "they" and "them," and some people use others (called neopronouns, or new pronouns), like "ze" and "hir." Some people use multiple pronouns like he/they, or they/she, or he/she, and some people use *any* pronouns. Folks who use multiple pronouns might list them in the order of their preference, and others don't care as much. Remember that all pronouns are valid. What might seem silly or superfluous to you might be the anchor for someone else's fundamental identity. Take these conversations slowly and follow your kid's lead, and work on developing a recurring *pronoun practice*.

You can do regular, even daily, pronoun check-ins with the young folks in your lives. You can also establish a regular practice for inviting young folks to share their pronouns with you, even if they fluctuate. This allows for flexibility and the potential for kids to change their minds, or experiment with different pronouns. All you have to do is ask: "What are your pronouns today?" Or: "What pronouns would you like me to use for you today?" It's that simple! You can—and should—reciprocate. Have them ask you the same question and respond with the pronouns you'd like them to use for *you* today.

There are lots of different ways we can incorporate being mindful of pronouns into our lives with kids, and also in our adult lives. Next time you introduce yourself to someone, tell them your name, and your pronouns, too! And make sure to ask for theirs, and model your consistent *pronoun practice* for others.

What's sneaky about talking to kids about pronouns is that we aren't introducing kids to an entirely new concept of gender; we're reframing a concept that they already understand and giving them language to describe it. When I go into schools and libraries for live performances, I like to start off the section of the performance on gender by asking if anyone in the audience knows what a pronoun is. Then I open it up to the room, and ask if anyone wants to share their pronouns. I always share mine first ("they/them!"), and I'll get a smattering of older kids who share with the group, and a grown-up or two if the crowd is warm enough. Getting everyone to practice and think about their pronouns, regardless of whether they are queer or nonbinary or trans, sets the groundwork for a queer-affirming environment.

Next—and this is my favorite part—I say that it can sometimes be a little scary sharing your pronouns with a big group of strangers, validating their emotions above all, and I invite the audience, on the count of three, to all shout their pronouns at once. I start the "Gender Song" amidst a cacophony of "he" and "she" and "they." The most important takeaway from this lesson is that gender isn't only about being a boy or being a girl, or being trans, or being nonbinary, it's about being true to your most authentic self, and proclaiming it to the world.

This process also subtly introduces the idea of nonbinary gender without fanfare. I'm talking about they/them pronouns in the same breath as binary gender pronouns (he/him and she/her). This makes sure that nonbinary identity doesn't get separated out; it doesn't get othered. It becomes *normalized* in conversations around gender. By positioning they/them pronouns up front within our definition of gender, we begin the work of dismantling the gender binary, or the idea that our gender can only be "boy" or "girl." This approach lays the groundwork for two important ideas: first, that gender lives on a spectrum rather than a binary, and second, that our gender identity is not defined by the gender we were assigned at birth.

YOUR DAILY PRONOUN PRACTICE

Here's a short example of a daily conversation practice you can start with your kids over something as simple as breakfast.

GROWN-UP

Good morning, sleepyhead! What cereal do you want today? Cheerios or Corn Flakes?

KID

Cheerios, please!

GROWN-UP

Here you go! What pronouns should I use for you today?

KID

Hmmm *(munch munch)* . . . Today's a he day!

GROWN-UP

Awesome! I'll use he/him/his for you today. Is it okay for me to use he for you around your friends and at school?

KID

Yup, that's okay! What are your pronouns today?

GROWN-UP

Today is a they day, thanks for asking!

KID

Yay for they!

It'll take you a few rounds of this to really get it into your system and routine, but it's truly as simple as that!

DRESS-UP AND DRAG

What's great about gender expression is that there are already established methodologies where kids can experiment: when they play dress-up! Dress-up and pretend play are *all about* creativity and experimentation, focusing on clothes and an expressive experimentation with gender. This is where dress-up meets drag.

You probably know about drag from *RuPaul's Drag Race* and the many, *many* Insta-famous queens running around the internet, or even from your local Drag Story Hour. But there's a whole heck of a lot more to drag than Ru's girls. Drag includes drag queens, drag kings, nonbinary drag performers, and trans drag performers! There are even cisgender women who perform as drag queens. Drag is an expansive art form that is defined solely by its theatricalization of gender expression, and not by so-called "cross-dressing." Drag is *gender performance* at its most visible.

Drag for kids—like Drag Story Hour—isn't exactly a new concept. It's simply been brought into a new age, thanks to the one and only Michelle Tea, a queer author and poet and the original creator of Drag Story Hour. In fact, drag has a surprisingly long history in Western children's theater. British pantomime (affectionately known as "panto") performances are vital—and unfortunately incredibly anti-trans—to the origin story of Western children's theater and media as we know it today. Children's theater as a whole has a long history—for better or worse—of cross-dressing gender performance: think of the women who've played Peter Pan for centuries or the (anti-trans) man-in-a-dress trope that's all over children's media. I had to turn off the first *Paddington* movie (of all things!) because of a man-in-a-dress scene featuring transmisogyny and trans panic, two tropes that actively harm real life trans women because they perpetuate anti-trans stereotypes.[18] It's an incredibly thin line between harmful anti-trans cross-dressing tropes and drag that celebrates and artfully theatricalizes gender expression.

The actual art form of drag—which I consider simply another form of dress-up—is a fantastic way for kids to experiment with their gender expression. Exposing kids to drag performances shows them that gender expression can meet creativity, and that gender can be fun and wacky and whimsical and push boundaries. It doesn't have to be such a serious business! Going one step further and actively encouraging kids to express themselves through drag with clothes and makeup and theatricality gives them agency, as well as a means to test out their gender expression and celebrate it.

One thing to remember is that gender expression does not always correlate to gender identity. There are some AMAB (assigned male at birth) kids who love to wear dresses and florals and flowy fabrics who lean more feminine, but they ultimately identify as cisgender boys, and not as trans girls. There are some AFAB (assigned female at birth) kids who love to wear overalls and baseball caps and lean more masculine but are nonbinary (like me!), and are not binary trans men. Drag is a great way to explore gender expression, but that expression can look very different from our gender identity.

A kid who figures out their gender expression through creativity and experimentation might start to learn more about their gender identity, but they also might not. It's important to understand how gender identity and gender

18 If you're at all curious about anti-trans tropes in media, check out the incredible documentary *Disclosure* that tackles trans representation in television and film!

expression are distinct components. Dress-up and drag are merely the sandbox. Eventually, they'll have experimented and tried things enough times that they will start to understand what kind of gender expression feels *euphoric* to them.

CLOTHING STORES

Let's move away from drag and gender performance and into the clothing aisle. These spaces, much like toy aisles, are *highly* gendered. When you step into any clothing store (physical or virtual, for kids or adults), gender confronts you immediately: in the distinct sections, separate dressing rooms, different color schemes—everything.

But clothes are objects. They are stitched textiles. Objects and textiles do not have gender—only things that are *alive* have genders. We are social animals who project associations onto everything. That's all fine and dandy, but the problem arises when we assign *strict gendered rules* to our clothes, as in "Boys can't wear dresses" or "That shirt is in the boys' section and you're a girl, so you can't wear it!" The gender assigned to clothing is about historical precedent, capitalism, and oppressive patriarchal standards of beauty and gender roles. Clothes have gender because we are told they have gender, not because they inherently have gender. Florals can be feminine, but they can be masculine, too; it depends on their context! We must constantly work to detach clothes from the notion of rigid gender, especially with kids.

If we can walk into a clothing store (or browse them virtually) and see the gendered aisles, we can *choose* to ignore those markers. We can show young people that they can find the clothing that they *enjoy,* rather than forcing them to fit into the clothing that has been designated for them by an executive at a clothing company. I have always had a lot of anxiety around clothes shopping as a trans nonbinary person. This started when I was a tween and has continued into my adult years. It's become easier as I've eschewed the "men's" and "women's" sections in lieu of exploring the full store and what fits my fancy. The trauma runs deep, but you can avoid creating this trauma for the kids in your care. Let your AFAB kid run wild in the "boy's section" and let your AMAB kid wear dresses and skirts if they want to! All you have to do is show them that they don't have to stick to the arbitrary clothing rules. No rules! How fun is that?!

Take the principles about drag and dress-up that you are reinforcing at home and apply them to the clothing aisle. Tell your kids to ignore the signs that say "boy's" and "girl's," and let them know that they can go anywhere in the store to find the clothes that they like. Do this for yourself as well! The next time you are clothes shopping, take a look at what the other section has going on. I personally always love the options for graphic T-shirts and button-downs in the men's section, while I get my jeans from the women's section. Maybe you'll learn something new about yourself that you love. You never know!

TOY STORES

Hand in hand with the gendered-ness of clothing stores is the toy aisle. Barbies are for girls and action figures are for boys. If society doesn't drive this message home through kid-targeted advertising, then the toy aisle definitely does, no question about it. If you want to avoid the toy aisle altogether, stick to online shopping, especially at independent retailers and shops, but digital shopping spaces haven't yet escaped gendered menus and categories. Seek out toy companies that are actively working against gendered aisles—LEGO is good at this, and Mattel's Creatables are a decent option, too. Mattel even came out with a Barbie doll version of trans icon Laverne Cox! But you can also repeat practices from the clothing section and have a direct conversation with your kid, reinforcing that you don't care what aisle the toy they want comes from. Toys, like clothes, are objects; they don't inherently have a gender.

Clothes and toys are by far the most explicit spaces where the gender binary is impressed upon young children, so it is up to you to work against those forces to give kids language that actively works against the oppression of these particular spaces.

BOYS WHO WEAR DRESSES AND TOXIC MASCULINITY

Let's talk for a moment about boys in dresses.

When I spoke with Seth Day, a queer trans man, educator, full-time nanny, and former host of the show *Rad Child Podcast,* he mentioned that, in all his years as a queer and trans nanny and caretaker, he makes a point to ask the parents he works with if it is okay for him to dress their babies and toddlers in whatever clothes they want. The parents usually give a casual "yes, that's totally fine," but in practice, he says he has been asked to sit down for a *talk* with multiple families after he put their AMAB baby in a dress, no matter whether the parents are straight or gay or trans themselves. Routinely, when Day puts the AMAB child—we're talking about an infant who can't make conscious decisions about their own clothes here—in a dress, the parents have had a problem with it. (Whereas, putting an AFAB infant in any clothes from a dress to cargo pants? Completely fine.)

This is a symptom of toxic masculinity, and a particularly rough byproduct of an inherently misogynist, patriarchal society that keeps boys and men from expressing themselves as anything that could be perceived as feminine. This pervasive ideology leads people to police and dictate masculine behavior in men and masculine people; encouraging men to be aggressive, stoic, tough (mentally and physically), heterosexual, staunchly independent, and insensitive, among many other toxic traits and behaviors. We project toxic masculinity onto our children, especially young boys—that's where that voice that might be in your head comes from, which shouts, "Boys can't wear dresses!"

There is nothing about dresses that is inherently female or feminine. Dresses might be perceived as feminine *nowadays*, but that is a human projection onto inanimate objects. Men have worn dresses throughout history! The perception that dresses are inherently feminine is a modern idea. In fact, most humans—men and women alike—wore some form of dress or skirt throughout ancient history; think of ancient Greek and Roman togas. The oldest known pair of pants came from somewhere between the thirteenth and tenth centuries BCE in present-day Western China, and they had nothing to do with gender. They were worn to protect a person's legs while they were horseback riding. So what exactly is so bad about boys who want to wear dresses? If you have a baby or toddler who is assigned male, why not try seeing if they might like to wear a dress?

There was a fantastic video that went viral where a boy wanted to dress up like Elsa from *Frozen* but was nervous about what people would think, so his dad got the same adult-sized version of the Elsa dress and wore it around with his son. That is the kind of gender-affirming parenting I'm talking about! Work through and unpack your internalized toxic masculinity and let your AMAB kid try on a dress. If you're still not sure about your assigned boy wearing a dress, try having him wear it at home and slowly work your way out of the house with it, if he likes wearing it; he might need to take baby steps with it, too. But if it's something you are approaching with fear because of your own hang-ups and you aren't following your child at the pace they want to go, then you are actively keeping them from expressing themselves and their gender, and that can turn into shame. That is not the work of spreading queer joy.

DEPROGRAMMING TRANSMISOGYNY

Reflect for a moment and ask yourself what would you do if your AMAB child wanted to wear a dress? How would you feel? Would you begrudgingly say yes, or would you give them your enthusiastic support? Would you feel *funky* about it? Would you worry about your spouse/co-parent's reaction? Or your own parent's judgment? Or your friends'? What if an AMAB[19] student walked into your classroom or school wearing a dress? How would you support that child? Ask yourself these hard questions, work to disrupt your own internalized toxic masculinity and transmisogyny,

---

19 I'm using the acronyms "AMAB" and "AFAB" here quite a bit to illustrate a point about transmisogyny largely experienced by AMAB transfemmes, but these designations can be harmful and overused. A good rule of thumb is to never ask a trans or nonbinary person their assigned gender—that's none of your business!

improve your ability to recognize when others perpetuate these ideas, and work on ways you can interrupt those situations if you feel safe enough to do so.

WHAT TO DO WHEN . . . A KID SAYS, "YOU CAN'T WEAR THAT, DRESSES ARE FOR GIRLS!"

Here's a teachable moment if there ever was one! When a kid uses a learned binary norm to tell another kid or person what they can and cannot do because of their gender, they are gifting you an opportunity to undo their limited worldview. This is a fantastic moment to take advantage of by digging deep. Here's how that conversation might go:

KID

You can't wear a dress! You're a boy and dresses are for girls.

YOU

Why? Why can girls wear dresses and boys can't?

KID

Because they can't! They're not allowed.

YOU

That doesn't sound very fair to me that only girls can wear dresses and boys can't. Does that sound fair to you?

KID
Hmmm, I guess not.

YOU
And I like wearing dresses! They make me feel good. What if I told you that girls *and* boys can wear dresses if they want to?

KID
Then . . . I guess it's okay for you to wear a dress. I'm gonna go play now. Bye!

You can adapt this script to your situation whether you're the one breaking the gender norm or it's another child or a stranger passing by. You probably won't get into a bigger conversation around gender here because confronting these kinds of biases can be a lot for a kid in the moment. Remember to move through any discomfort you might be feeling with patience and understanding. Listening to where a child is coming from is *key* in these situations!

GENDER ASSIGNMENT AND DOLLS

It is a truth universally acknowledged that babies love babies. Babies are *obsessed* with other babies! This is one of many reasons why dolls make up an enormous section of every toy aisle and have so for as long as we've mass manufactured toys.

For this reason, it makes perfect sense to use the baby

dolls that are probably already in your house—that your child knows and loves—to dismantle ideas around gender assignment and pronouns. If your child doesn't have a doll, you can also do this exercise with a beloved stuffy.

Using your toddler's doll, you can engage them in thinking about whether or not they've already assigned a gender to their doll. If they have, prompt a conversation about why they assigned that particular gender. (This is also a great opportunity to use accurate body language!) Maybe you and your child use imaginary play to ask their doll their gender. You could start by asking why they might have chosen their doll's name. If they think their doll is a boy or a girl or neither or both—why? What pronouns does their doll want to use and why? What are their doll's favorite clothes? The list goes on and on, and you can tailor it to your kid's specific play style. This exercise gets kids to think through their assumptions about gender—and lays the groundwork for ideas around transness versus cisness—in a way that is accessible and impacts one of their favorite things: their beloved doll (or stuffy)!

This is also a great way to continue pronoun practice with your child. Make room to ask your child *and* their doll about their pronouns, and allow those pronouns to shift and change; affirm their pronouns no matter what they are, and no matter if they change again. When I spoke with Seth Day, he told a story of a boy he nannied who woke up from a nap one day and wanted to be called Gabby and use she/her pronouns, which is what Seth did for a full week. Then, the boy said that he wanted to be called Timothy again and went back to he/him pronouns. What's the harm in that? So what if it is a phase? What that child got out of that week of trying a new name and pronouns was the knowledge that no matter what his gender or pronouns are, he would be affirmed in his gender identity and taken seriously by the adults in his life. That's absolutely worthwhile.

PIVOTING AWKWARD QUESTIONS

Preschoolers in particular are naturally curious and are *not* shy about asking questions that might be embarrassing or uncomfortable, and situations might arise that you don't necessarily know how to deal with. Let's go over a few strategies for dealing with these awkward moments.

Trystan Reese—a white gay trans dad, influencer, executive coach, consultant, and author of *How We Do Family*—spoke with me about the ways he and his husband raise their kids queerly, and how he deals with difficult situations head-on. He told me a story about his four-year-old son, Leo, who overheard the family behind them in line at T.J. Maxx speaking Spanish. Leo turned around, pointed at them, and said, "They're not speaking English." (I'm sure you've been in a similar situation with your child before when they noticed something *different*.) Instead of telling Leo to shush or getting embarrassed, Trystan engaged with Leo and questioned his question: "Yes, they're speaking another language, can you tell what language they are speaking?" Trystan was able to turn what might have been an awkward situation into a learning opportunity. The family was gracious in this moment and joined in the conversation and told Leo, "We're speaking Spanish!"

These moments are nerve-racking. We want to mitigate harm to those around us, but we also need to address these curiosities, because kids ask questions and express themselves when their understanding of the world is disrupted. In these moments, we can see where we need to do more work ourselves, to show young folks a world that is more diverse so they won't have these questions—where a kid like Leo already knows that some families might speak different languages. These are learning opportunities for kids, but also for their grown-ups, to see where their work falls short.

Leo's story is an example of how we can work to build understanding of difference and learn to celebrate it, rather than push the curiosity away out of embarrassment. Do your best to turn moments where you might feel like you are experiencing a failure in your child-rearing into a teachable moment and a rich learning opportunity. And it is important to *engage* above all, because this disruption won't only happen with families behind us in line at T.J. Maxx who speak different languages. This happens with trans women when kids ask their parents, "Why is that man wearing a dress?" It happens with Black folks whose hair texture might look different to a white child who hasn't had much exposure to Black communities. It happens in response to all kinds of difference, and all kinds of queerness. You have to engage with these disruptions in order to turn that difference from something that's weird or strange into something that is beautiful. Remember: different is *awesome*.

WHAT TO DO WHEN . . . YOUR KID ASKS ABOUT SOMEONE'S BODY

This connection between our gender identity, gender expression, and our bodies has been a sticking point for much of society and for the relationships between children and trans people in particular. Young children often feel the dissonance between the binary-gendered world peddled to them and first learning about trans, nonbinary, and queer people. A young person's curiosity around the mixed messages they are hearing might prompt them to ask invasive questions of trans and nonbinary people that can be hurtful to them, even if there is no malintent. This invasiveness tends to make trans and nonbinary adults nervous around children.

Questions from children like "Why is that man wearing a dress?" are not intentionally trying to cause discomfort; rather, the child is trying to reconcile what they understand about gender and its perceived connection to our bodies. It is important for cis people not to be scared of answering these important questions! Here's a great opportunity to start teaching appropriate boundaries and rules of privacy. People's bodies are their private business, and we shouldn't ask them about their bodies unless they explicitly give their consent or permission. You can even hearken back to the conversations you had around consent in toddlerhood.

This situation is one that trans and nonbinary people face far too often when their bodies become the subject of interrogation, when trans and nonbinary people should be able to set their own boundaries of privacy around their bodies. It is vital that cisgender folks are literate in these concepts so that they can properly answer young people's questions without placing the emotional burden and labor on trans and nonbinary people.

TACKLING SEXUALITY
Those are the gender basics! There's more to come on gender, but we'll wait until the kids are a bit older to get more specific. Let's segue into conversations around sexuality. I'll reiterate that gender and sexuality are completely different—but connected—topics entirely. Let's make sure we handle them as separate conversations as we introduce concepts of gender and sexuality to our pre-K kids.

WHAT DOES GAY MEAN?
The reason we covered gender before sexuality is because sexuality can be a bit sticky. Kids understand and explore their gender identity at a very young age, but sexuality typically doesn't show up in their identity formation until they start going through puberty. There are definitely exceptions, and there are a lot of queer people who have incredibly early memories of their emerging sexualities. But still, the question arises: Why do they need to understand sexuality at such a young age?

This question is shortsighted, because information around sexuality isn't simply about helping kids develop their own sexuality. It's about reinforcing, from the start, that heterosexuality isn't the *only* possible sexuality out there. Look at any Disney movie from *Snow White* to *Aladdin* to *Tangled*, *The Princess and the Frog*, and *Frozen*. Every single one of those movies revolves around (or at least includes) a significant heterosexual romance and love story central to the overall plot of the film. Even children's media isn't immune to the societal pressures of heterosexuality.

Heterosexuality is front and center, and we need to show kids other possibilities. Take the so-called nuclear family for instance: a *man* and a *woman* and 2.5 kids. Romance

and romantic partnerships are foundational to societal structures. Adults make assumptions about children's future sexuality all the time. They even talk about how babies flirt
with babies of the opposite gender. Right now the predom-
inant narrative that exists says heterosexuality is the only
viable option. Breaking down the LGBTs and understanding
sexuality through gender and love allows us to talk about
sexuality in an age-relevant way.

GENDER + LOVE = SEXUALITY

Here's where the layering starts. Since we already have a
working understanding of gender, we can use it to build an understanding of sexuality. But we can't explain sexuality with
gender alone; something is still missing. So, we go back under
the doorknob to see if we can find something to give sexuality
context for a child. There, we find two things: (1) love and (2)
family. Our way *in* is through understanding different family
structures. There's a simple equation we can work with:

$$\text{Gender} + \text{Love} = \text{Sexuality}$$

Simply put, your sexuality puts a label on the kind of people you love, namely their gender. I use the word "love" a bit
vaguely here for the sake of simplicity. You can go deeper and
get into different kinds of love, like love between grown-ups
(generally, that's romantic love) versus love between friends
(platonic) versus love in a family (familial). However, when
you're first starting these conversations, it's easy to stick to
the basics: some boys love boys, some boys love girls, some
girls love girls, some girls love boys, and some people love
boys and girls and nonbinary people. It's really that simple!
Conceptually, there isn't a lot more to sexuality. The em-

phasis here is on the fact that love is beautiful, and we should celebrate it in all its forms. In the words of Lin Manuel-Miranda, "Love is love is love is love." And sexuality is all about who we love. Where it can get complicated is in all the different vocabulary folks might use to label their sexuality. We'll look at some of those labels when we break down the LGBTQ+ acronym, but let's find our way in with family structures first.

DIFFERENT KINDS OF FAMILIES

While young children might not have developed sexualities of their own, they are surrounded by grown-ups who have, and those sexualities are often represented in their family's visible structure. Families can be made up of a mom and a dad and their children, but families can also have two moms, or two dads, or a mom and a baba (one of many terms of endearment for a nonbinary parent), or a dad and a baba; or a trans dad who carried and birthed their child; or multiple parents potentially in polyamorous relationships or practicing co-parenting within a community; stepparents, or grandparents, or aunts, uncles, siblings, cousins, chosen family, etc. Making the link from queer sexuality to queer family structures helps kids understand sexuality in an immediate way, because who's closer to their experiences than the people they are around the most in their lives?

CONVERSATION STARTER: WORDS FOR NONBINARY PARENTS AND RELATIVES

When it comes to families, most of the words we use to describe our relationships are gendered, so many queer, nonbinary, and trans people have to get creative and decide what they want to be called for themselves.

There are lots of different nonbinary terms and names that folks might use. If you know someone who is queer, trans, or nonbinary, make sure you ask them what they want to be called. Instead of mom or dad, some nonbinary parents are baba; ren or renny, which is short for p*arent*; or maddy (mommy + daddy). Sibling is a great alternative to "sister" or "brother." Cousin is gender neutral all by itself, but a nonbinary person might prefer a word like "nibling" instead of "niece" or "nephew."

Have a conversation about what words feel good to the people in your life before you make any assumptions, like we've practiced with pronouns. And don't forget to talk to your kids about the words they should use for the loved ones in their lives!

As you can see, alternate family structures are not unique to queer families. We can reshuffle kids' ideas of what a family might look like by talking about lots of different structures, including queer families. Across different cultural practices, it is perfectly normal for multiple generations to live under the same roof, to be close to extended family members, and to include the unique makeup of blended families. This moves into anti-racist practices in decentralizing narratives around *white and Christian* family structures, which we'll talk about when we get to intersectionality.

Even though my parents are straight and cis, I grew up in a complicated blended family when my parents divorced, remarried, and I gained two stepsisters. Our *Brady Bunch* setup wasn't always the easiest to navigate (within my immediate family there are a grand total of five different last names), and seeing my family's experience reflected in *modern* stories might have made things a little bit easier to navigate. Since my stepsisters and I were similar ages, we all went to the same high school together, but the school's administration couldn't figure out why we were siblings with different last names. Our complicated family consistently confounded people, and my family wasn't even queer!

This is where normalizing different family structures is so important, especially for kids from queer families, because it becomes more and more difficult for them to navigate the world when everyone around them assumes that their family can only look one way. When I spoke with Trystan about his experience as a gay trans dad, he noted the painful interactions he's witnessed his son experience when kids—even those from well-meaning and accepting liberal families—ask him why he doesn't have a mommy, and if his mommy is dead. We need to expand our understanding of what families can look like, and we can do that by *talking about it* with young people. With a greater understanding of sexuality that extends beyond heteronormativity, we can give kids the tools to understand not only their own family structure, but their friends' families, too.

So talk to your preschoolers about different kinds of families! Make sure you have books that show different family structures and be sure to point them out and make observations about those depictions with your kids at bedtime or your classroom's story time. The possibility of queer sexuality comes second nature to kids born into queer families, but they so rarely see their families reflected or acknowledged by the world around them. This is the work of validation for kids who grow up in queer family structures—whether they turn out to be queer themselves or not—and nurturing young allies with an understanding of the world that does not explicitly center white straight family narratives.

AN INTRODUCTION TO ACTIVISM AND SOCIAL JUSTICE

Now that we have built the fundamentals around aspects of our identity, we can place them in context with the world. As we move beyond gender and sexuality to start conversations around other aspects of our identities like race, class, disability, and more, we can help kids layer different aspects of their identities on top of each other, understand how they fit into the world, and nurture a sense of justice. Moving toward an understanding of larger justice-centered topics is the organic progression from an interrogation of gender, sexuality, and identity because children have to exist *in the world* in their identities, same as us grown-ups. Don't get hung up on words that seem too big for kids like "intersectionality." Remember, don't underestimate small humans because they're small.

WHAT IS INTERSECTIONALITY?

What I love about queerness is that it is ubiquitous. There are LGBTQ+ people across cultures, countries, race, ethnicity, class, religion, disability—the list goes on. And every other facet of identity intersects with queerness in its own way. No one person is only one thing! I am not only queer, I am not only white, I am not only Jewish, I am not only trans, I am not one facet of my identity alone. Noted Black critical race theory scholar and professor Kimberlé Crenshaw coined the term "intersectionality" to describe this idea around our identities: that we are greater than the sum of our parts. In her seminal essay "Demarginalizing the Intersection of Race and Sex," she introduces intersectionality to describe Black women's specific oppression as one that cannot be described by either misogyny or racism alone. Her theory suggests that Black women feel the *intersecting* effects of *both* misogyny and racism simultaneously. In an interview, she describes intersectionality as a "lens through which you can see where power comes and collides, where it interlocks and intersects. It's not simply that there's a race problem here, a gender problem here, a class or LBGTQ [sic] problem there. Many times that framework erases what happens to people who are subject to all of these things." In other words, her theory can be applied widely to anyone who experiences multiple intersections of oppression like anti-trans, anti-queer, and other marginalizations. Intersectionality describes the way a person can experience compounding oppressive forces in their life.

We have to look at our whole selves to understand how we move through the world, where we have the power and privilege to open doors for others, and where we have to fight and speak out about injustices we experience to make them visible. Where I have privilege in my whiteness, physical ability, and access to wealth and education in my youth, I am marginalized in my queerness, transness, Jewishness, and neurodivergence. We can use our privileges in comradery to uplift and fight for others, and we can look to our marginalizations for community and spaces where we might be disadvantaged and can speak out to make change.

In fact, your approach to the lessons and topics in this book might look completely different to another reader *because* of intersectionality. Maybe you live in a bilingual household and you need to talk about pronouns and gender in two different languages. Or maybe you come from a religious background and are a person of faith, and want to talk to your child about how you reconcile your faith with queer identity. Those are some big things to think about! You come to this work from your own unique perspective.

The work of queer liberation cannot be done in isolation from other movements because of the inherent nature of queerness. Queer liberation is liberation for *all*. We need to show young kids that there are queer people who are *exactly like them*. There are white queer and trans people, there are Black queer and trans people, there are Brown queer and trans people, there are Asian queer and trans people, there are disabled queer and trans people, there are poor queer and trans people, there are queer and trans autistic people, there are queer and trans people of faith, and there are people who are Black and disabled and poor and autistic and queer *and* trans. There are *all kinds* of queer and trans people, and every intersection of identity we make visible to young people helps them understand their identities individually and together. One day I hope there are as many different versions of this book as there are perspectives of folks who want to do this work.

So, uh, how exactly do we talk to preschoolers about intersectionality? This might sound complicated, and words like "intersectionality" might not feel accessible for young folks, but we've already got the building blocks. This concept is all about putting what we've already learned together to form a larger picture. These are, to be sure, more advanced topics, but you'll be surprised what kids can comprehend when you don't underestimate them. Once we understand each part of our identity, it becomes obvious that we have to take them all into account at once, instead of separately. You can easily layer these conversations around gender and sexuality alongside conversations you are hopefully also having about race, class, disability, etc. We'll get more specific about the conversations you should be having around these identities when we get to kindergarten, but you should already be organically embedding them in the queer work you're doing. Take extra care to make sure the materials you are using are mindful of intersectionality in depictions of all different kinds of queer identity! If you are exposing kids to diverse experiences of queerness, then you're already helping them recognize people and characters with multifaceted identities. Tackling intersectionality with kids is a heck of a lot easier when you've already had these conversations. You've already done the heavy lifting!

PRIVILEGE AND FAIRNESS

We've discussed the idea of privilege, but let's talk about it as a specific concept. Privilege is really a word for telling us how the structures of society perceive and treat us based on our (many) identities. We can talk about privilege as it relates to specific parts of our identity and where different people have and lack privilege, but what does that mean?

Put simply, we have systemic privilege in society where any one of our identities isn't marginalized. For example, a white person has privilege because they do not experience oppressive systemic racism like a Black, or Brown, or Asian, or Native person does. And a straight person has privilege because they don't experience systemic anti-queer and anti-gay biases. And a cisgender person has privilege because they don't experience systemic anti-trans discrimination. And so on and so forth.

When we talk about this idea with kids, I like to lean on fairness, a value that young folks understand intimately.

You've read about childism in the earlier chapters, and that is where fairness can really hit home. Children lack privilege specifically because of childism. Children can pinpoint practically where they might feel the *unfairness* of childism in their day-to-day lives: the lack of control they might have over their schedule, grown-ups in their lives dismissing their wants and needs and opinions, grown-ups withholding important information. Even punishments they might receive because of "bad behavior." Children have an acute understanding of fairness because of childism.

Young kids don't generally have a whole lot of independence in their lives. They have choice, and some forms of autonomy, but generally, they live at the behest of you all, the grown-ups in their lives, and that means that the decisions we make for them might not always seem fair from their perspective. It's important that we make instances of unfairness—or sometimes oppression, racism, anti-gay and anti-trans sentiments—transparent to young people.

Imagine a set of monkey bars on a playground. Tall kids with long arms might swing from bar to bar without any problems. But a shorter child with shorter arms might not even be able to reach the first bar, let alone swing easily to the next one. But the problem doesn't lie in the height difference between these two kids. It is about the monkey bars themselves not being accessible to everyone.

Beyond that metaphor, you can have conversations with your kids about why some people are not treated fairly by others because of who they are. Kids have *powerful* imaginations, and we can encourage them to view privilege and identity not as a competition or "oppression Olympics" or as a pity party, but as an opportunity to take a look at the realities of our world and imagine a better future and figure out, collectively, how to turn that vision into a reality. So, how can we build a jungle gym that's truly for *everyone*? How can we create a jungle gym where everybody wins? Where no matter your identity, you have the same opportunities as everyone else? Where everyone has a future that is *fair*? We'll come back around to this idea when we discuss equality, equity, and justice.

WHAT IS SOCIAL JUSTICE?

Let's back up a second and look at what activism actually is.

You've probably heard the phrase "social justice" thrown around a lot, but what does it mean? When we talk about social justice, we're talking about pretty much every social system we encounter as humans; our communication pathways, our economy, our government, our arts sectors, our education, the list goes on and on. Social *justice* speaks to the ways these structures and systems are unfair and oppressive, and looks for ways to fix or rebuild them. But what does that entail on a practical level, and how can we talk to kids about such a large topic? Let's break it down into smaller chunks.

Justice is how we evaluate fairness. (You can see how all of these ideas weave together, especially when you're talking to kids!) Throughout history, as far back as ancient Egypt in 2400 BCE, justice has been symbolized by a scale weighing two things against each other. In ancient Egyptian mythology, when a person died and their spirit left their body, they would pass through the Hall of Judgment where they met Ma'at, the god of truth, balance, justice, and order. The person's heart would be weighed against Ma'at's feather of truth, and if the scale was perfectly balanced, they could continue on to the afterlife. Our modern concept of justice isn't so far off.

Justice uses this metaphorical scale to see whether something is in balance. When things are in balance, they are fair; when things are out of balance, they are unfair! You see how we keep coming back to this idea of fairness that kids can grasp? It's how we can frame all of these conversations so they can understand big ideas, like social justice, in their own terms. When we talk specifically about *social* justice, we're measuring that fairness in the context of our society. It's a pursuit where we strive toward shifting society so that the metaphorical scales balance out, and we reach true equity among all people.

Modern social justice movements recognize that the scales are way out of balance. Our society does not treat people fairly because of their race, ethnicity, gender, sexuality, ability status, socioeconomic status, religion, and a whole lot of other factors. We fight for social justice in pursuit of fairness for everyone, regardless of their identity, and for balance in our society. The methodology for working within social justice movements to balance the scales and attempt to fix inequity is called activism.

WHAT IS ACTIVISM?

If the first step is to recognize that the scales of justice are out of balance, then the next step is to figure out how to fix them with an understanding of activism and becoming an activist. Like in earlier chapters, we're building a daily practice. This time, it's your activism practice, which you can create for yourself *and* your family, classroom, library, etc.

I realized early on in creating *Queer Kid Stuff* that I couldn't only talk about gender and sexuality. The reality of queerness is that there is great joy but there is also great oppression and suffering. The only way to fight for that joy is by being an activist—or someone who takes action to change something they care about.

There are lots of different ways to be an activist. You can use your words and art; you can organize book drives, contribute resources to unhoused people, and participate in a protest. You can do all of those things, you can do some, or only one. They *all* make you an activist. If you're reading this book, chances are that you are *already* an activist, even if you don't realize it yet. All you have to do is shift from passive bystander and observer to become an *active* participant in the justice movements you are already learning about. Let's look at one way to practically approach these ideas with kids!

MAKING PROTEST SIGNS

Take your first step toward activism with the young person in your life: make a protest sign! Grab some art supplies—a piece of cardboard or a few pieces of paper, and crayons, markers, paint, whatever you have lying around—and get started.

First, have a conversation about what a protest is and what kind of protest your signs are for. Protests are a physical form of activism where organizers bring people together to march or rally at a particular location and voice feelings like passion, anger, frustration, and sadness about something unjust. Ask yourself, what is happening in the news right now that you feel passionately about? Are you advocating for LGBTQ+ rights, Black lives, climate change, or reproductive rights? Maybe there's something happening in your local community that's a little closer to home, like a local politician who's doing something you don't like, or a school that's getting closed down, or a company that isn't treating its workers well? Whatever it is, the only requirement is that you *care* about it—and you don't have to pick only one!

Once you've settled on a topic, go to town. Grab those crayons and markers and paints and get creative. As you work, talk about why you care about the topic you picked, and why you chose to represent it the way you did on your sign. Then present your completed signs to each other and talk about the images or phrases you chose and why they resonate with you. Maybe they're funny! Maybe they hit on a specific angle. Don't be afraid to really dig into it.

Then, take the signs to real protests in your local area, or stage a protest at home with your family. This might feel a bit safer, and it's still an excellent stepping stone for *practicing activism*. March around your house or apartment, even your block if you're adventurous, and show your kids what it feels like to march for something you care about. When you're done, display the signs in your space, either on your walls, your fridge, your windows, or even the lawn. Practice and model being proud and open about your activism in order to nurture theirs. Activism won't feel so overwhelming after this, I guarantee it!

REFLECTION

Wow, we covered a *lot* of topics with our preschoolers: We laid the foundation for their understanding of gender, sexuality, even intersectionality and activism. We learned about gender euphoria, considered how pronouns communicate our gender identity, broke down ways we can navigate rigid gender structures in clothing and toy stores, and worked through sticky situations we might encounter as we dismantle the gender binary. We learned a simple equation to help us explain sexuality and looked at a bunch of different family structures. We started to put our identities together with an understanding of fairness and privilege through a preliminary definition of intersectionality that finally got us to the beginning of our journey as activists. And you learned that kids as young as three are completely capable of understanding these ideas. It's time for us to graduate and officially enter kindergarten!

KEY TAKEAWAYS

- Age three is a *crucial* year to introduce topics like gender and sexuality to your kids because they are starting to establish their sense of self.

- Pronouns are a fantastic way to start the conversation around gender, but they're not the end-all be-all.

- Gender + Love = Sexuality

- Don't underestimate small humans because they are small. Intersectionality isn't too big of a word for pre-K kids.

- Don't forget to go under the doorknob! Focus on terms and ideas that kids can understand like fairness, love, and even something as relatable as the monkey bars!

Part V

ELEMENTARY SCHOOLERS (AGES 4+)

THE FIRST DAY OF KINDERGARTEN

Get the camera ready—we're off to elementary school! This section is large in scope and spans well beyond four- and five-year-olds. You'll more than likely use these lessons through your kids' tween and high school years as they continue to grapple with their sense of self in the context of modern society. This section is about digging in and getting really specific with our vocabulary, parsing out more nuanced ideas of justice, and navigating queer history. Let's jump right in!

A FEW THINGS TO REMEMBER ABOUT ELEMENTARY SCHOOLERS

- They're ready for bigger words and more complicated topics now! Don't get nervous that a concept is too big or hard. Let them lead the way.

- Make sure you're guiding them to learn things on their own beyond your own conversations with them.

> • When in doubt, it's always better to ask questions. We're paying more attention to detail now!

REVISITING GENDER

Until now, we've only dabbled in specific vocabulary around gender. You've read about gender identity, expression, and euphoria, and have definitions for intersectionality, social justice, and activism. But it's time we take a closer look at the words we can use to describe ourselves and our identities, particularly when it comes to gender and sexuality. We'll also move beyond gender and sexuality to look at and *name* all of our identities and help kids understand themselves as whole humans. But first, let's further define some things we've already talked about, like *nonbinary* identity and the *gender spectrum*.

NONBINARY GENDER AND THE GENDER SPECTRUM

Now that they're older, it's time to pair words with the bigger concepts and make everything clearer.

First, let's address with kids what it means to identify as *nonbinary*. You can start by using an example that's familiar to the age group, like counting. Take the number two. Another way we represent the number two through our words is with the letters "B" and "I." We put the prefix "bi" in front of a word to show it has to do with the number two, like how *bi*cycles have two wheels.

When we talk about *bi*nary gender that means we are talking about *two* genders, boys and girls. The binary gender system that we live in says that there are only boys and girls, men and women, male and female. But we already know that's not true! Return to your shared understanding of pronouns; some people use he/him pronouns, some people use she/her pronouns, some people use they/them pronouns, some people use neopronouns like ze/hir, and some people use multiple pronouns! There is way more to human gender identity than these two prescriptive boxes of boys and girls. All of those different pronouns show us that there is a whole *spectrum* of gender that exists between and outside of these two binary genders, and anyone—and I mean *anyone*—who identifies in the space between and/or outside of those two binary genders is usually considered nonbinary (affectionately "enby," from the vocalization of the acronym NB—which you shouldn't use on its own because it means "non-Black").

There's a *lot* of space outside of the binary boxes of boy and girl. That means that there are infinite ways to be nonbinary! You don't have to explain every infinite version of nonbinary-ness to your child because that would likely be overwhelming, but if they ask, you can tell them there are nonbinary women, there are nonbinary men, there are people who are simply nonbinary; there are agender folks who don't identify as having a gender at all who may or may not feel like they are under the nonbinary umbrella; there are bigender folks who are *both* male and female; there are genderfluid, genderqueer, and gender creative folks; there are demiboys and demigirls. The limit truly does not exist. There are *plenty* of resources online with definitions for specific nonbinary labels and identities that you and your kid can explore together—see page 225.

So you see, we're not introducing anything new here, we're simply naming something we already understand to be true. This is all part of the work of dismantling the binary gender system we all live in, grew up in, and are accustomed to.[20] Follow your kid's lead—as always—and do your best to answer their questions. This is a fantastic time to learn alongside your kid and discover gender identities you might not have been aware of before. Co-learning is a pretty cool way to bond with your kid. Don't be scared to give it a try!

NONBINARY IDENTITY ISN'T NEW

Nonbinary and trans people have existed throughout all of recorded history—yes, *all*! The only reason why nonbinary and trans identities feel so new is because of colonization. Others have written about this at length (and you can see more resources on page 225), but in a nutshell, rigid gender roles passed down through settler colonialism have wreaked havoc on Indigenous cultures, particularly their more expansive understanding of human gender. The Jewish Talmud—a Rabbinical text documenting traditional Jewish law and theology—describes *eight* officially recognized genders. Two-spirit peoples existed in North American Native culture well before European colonization. Some Indigenous cultures recognize a third gender like India's hijra community, which holds a special and revered place in Hinduism and Native Hawaiian māhū people. The list goes on and on. Maybe *your* cultural heritage might have

---

20 You might have noticed that in dismantling one binary (male and female) we have created a new binary system (binary and nonbinary), but that's a *whole other* conversation that is very much still being tossed around in contemporary discourse!

recognized a trans and/or nonbinary gender identity before settler colonialism. Take a poke around and see what you might find, or learn about an Indigenous gender identity you hadn't heard of before!

CISGENDER VS. TRANSGENDER

Like with the gender spectrum and nonbinary gender, "transgender" and "cisgender" aren't new terms for us because we've already established a foundation in the previous chapters. See why it's so important to start having these conversations from *womb to tomb*? It's not necessary to wait until kindergarten to tell your kids what it means to be trans—and you *should* definitely be using words like "trans" and "cis" around them from a very early age—but now is when they are more equipped developmentally to bring all these concepts together in order to fully grasp transness and cisness, as well as their unique definitions.

When I'm describing transgender and cisgender experiences to this age group, I usually start by talking about our assigned gender. In the earlier pages, you saw the acronyms AMAB and AFAB, which stand for *assigned male at birth* and *assigned female at birth*. We learned about gender assignments back when we talked about infants and gender reveal parties (*thumbs down emoji*). You can use the same definition to talk to your kids now by describing how doctors assign genders to babies based on their perception of that infant's body and genitals. Lean on any language you've already established with them, like how gender assignment is something that a doctor does to a kid without their *consent*. And you can practice using proper *body language,* too!

From there, you can explain the difference between being transgender and being cisgender. Cisgender people identify *with* their gender assigned at birth, and transgender (or trans) people do *not* identify with their gender assigned at birth. There are trans men, and trans women, and trans nonbinary people in the world, and they all fit snugly on the gender spectrum—bring that concept back around, too!—like all the other genders we've talked about. With everything we've already learned about gender—particularly gender assignment and consent—it makes perfect sense that some people might identify with their assigned gender and some might not. You can fold the concept of cis versus trans on top of conversations you've had around gender identity, expression, euphoria, and privilege.

It's essential to bring it all back to *feelings*. Ask your kid how someone who is trans might feel about their gender versus someone who is cisgender. Ask them how *they* feel about their assigned gender. Bring this conversation into your daily pronoun practice and talk about whether their pronouns that day align with their gender assignment. Does that mean they could be trans or could be cis? See how that makes them feel and let the conversation flow naturally with their curiosity. You might be surprised where they bring you!

The next step toward digging deeper into the trans experience with your kid is talking about *transition*. Transition is unique to the trans experience. It's when a trans person wants to change something about their body so that their external gender expression better matches their gender identity and brings them gender euphoria. Sometimes changing their hair or clothes might not be enough for a trans person

Rainbow Parenting   151

to feel gender euphoria in their body. That disjointedness might cause a trans person to feel gender *dysphoria*. A trans person might decide to transition in one way or another to find relief and better their mental health.

Not all trans people transition because they are dysphoric, but transitioning is a very important option to improve trans and nonbinary people's mental health. Some trans people get creative with their gender expression or wear specific kinds of clothes—like a compression binder, a tight-fitting bra-like undergarment folks with breasts might use to make their chests appear more masculine—to relieve feelings of gender dysphoria, but for some trans people it isn't enough. A trans person might also choose to medically transition in one way or another. They might take gender-affirming hormones or have gender-affirming surgery to feel more at home in their body. Transgender kids can take *hormone blockers* before they hit puberty so they can control—with a doctor's supervision—when and how they go through puberty in order to develop their body in a way that aligns with their gender identity.

Let's take a breath here for a moment. How are you feeling? What's your body doing as you read this section? Did you catch your breath when I mentioned talking to your kid about hormone blockers? If it did, that's okay! But consider these questions: Why does the idea of talking to your kid about hormone blockers elicit a physical reaction? How do you feel about the possibility that your child could be trans? How does it feel to give them crucial information about hormone blockers that could lead them on an important journey of self-discovery? How would you react if your child told you they were interested in talking to a doctor about hormone blockers?[21] Sit with those questions for as long as you need, and *before* you talk to your kid about hormone blockers or any other kind of transition. You need to bring your very best trans-affirming self to this conversation.

If your kid is cisgender, you can help them work through anti-trans bias and pass along important knowledge to your young cisgender ally. But if your kid is trans (whether you know it yet or not!), it could be one of the most important conversations in their young life. Be sure to work through your stuff *first* before you project any unconscious anti-trans sentiments onto them, wreaking havoc on their mental health and your relationship with them.

Let's move on to illustrate how I talk with kids about my own trans body and transition up to this point in my life. I feel a lot of gender euphoria around the clothes I wear, but it ultimately wasn't enough for me, so I decided to get top surgery—where a surgeon reshaped my chest to make it look more masculine—in January 2022. There are lots of different kinds of top surgeries, but the one I got left two large scars on my chest. I love my scars and take good care of them by massaging them and applying lots of sunscreen to help them heal and stay healthy. I love my new chest, but getting top surgery was a hard, and sometimes painful, experience. I am so much happier in my body and I am so glad I did it even though it was scary. I'm feeling really happy with my transition right now, but that might change in the

---

21 Hormone blockers or puberty blockers help young folks push the pause button on puberty until they feel ready to move forward (or not) with HRT (hormone replacement therapy) with their parents and medical team.

future. Transition might not have a starting or ending point for a trans person and that's totally okay!

WHAT DOES INTERSEX MEAN?

Something sad about the binary gender system we currently live in, and—if you're reading this book— are actively trying to dismantle, is that there are gendered expectations that come with our bodies. Our binary society dictates that "typical" boys and men have penises, and testicles, and "typical" girls and women have breasts, vulvas, vaginas, and uteruses. But this rigid perception of our bodies does not account for the expansive gender spectrum we've come to understand. This idea is especially important to remember when we talk about people who are intersex (the *I* in LGBTQIA!). People who are intersex do not have bodies that are easily categorized by the binary gender system, whether physically, biologically, chromosomally, or all three, proving that even our bodies exist on a spectrum. More often than not, intersex people are forced to undergo nonconsensual surgeries to "fix" their bodies when they are children. This practice must end.

What's important to note is that, even though some level of transition is right for many trans people, we must still work to dismantle the rigidity of binary gender that dictates our bodies. Men and women and nonbinary people can have penises, and testicles, and men and women and nonbinary people can have breasts, and vaginas, and uteruses, no matter their gender assignment. While many trans people opt to transition in some form or another, there isn't always an "endgame," or a final outcome of transitioning. For many, transitioning itself is a state of being that can shift and move to reflect where a person feels they are on the gender spectrum at any point in their life. But the most important point to drive home is that trans women are women, trans men are men, trans boys are trans boys, trans girls are trans girls, and nonbinary people are nonbinary, plain and simple. We must protect trans kids.

LEARN YOUR LGBTs

You've probably seen a lot of different versions of the acronym LGBT. We'll go through all of them here as a primer on some of the more common sexuality and gender identities you might come across. This list won't be exhaustive, but it's a good place to start, especially when you're introducing this vocabulary to your kindergartener!

Until now, we've been dealing with concepts like pronouns, gender identity, gender expression, and sexuality without a lot of emphasis on specific vocabulary, but don't be shy about using big words with small humans—this is all about exposure! That said, we also shouldn't underestimate kids (here's where we're continuing to attune ourselves to our childism biases): they probably understand more of these ideas than you'd think. Approach these conversations with curiosity and an open mind. I like to call this *learning our LGBTs*.

To start, we'll introduce two ideas to our kids: an acronym and an umbrella term. A kid-friendly definition of an acronym is "a word whose letters stand for other words." There are acronyms for things—SCUBA is an acronym that stands for Self-Contained Underwater Breathing

Apparatus—and there are acronyms for people: AOC stands for Alexandria Ocasio-Cortez. There are acronyms for organizations—NASA stands for National Aeronautics and Space Administration—and there are even acronyms for actions: LOL stands for Laugh Out Loud! We use acronyms as a shorthand for something that is a bit of a mouthful. There are also acronyms for an entire community, like LGBT.

This particular acronym is doing double duty—it is also what we call an umbrella term. For kids, an umbrella term is a word we use to represent a lot of different words, identities, even people. It's not hard to imagine Teddy and I sitting under a giant rainbow umbrella in the *Queer Kid Stuff* episode where we talk about LGBTQ+ as a literal umbrella term! The acronym LGBTQ+ is an umbrella term for everyone who identifies as lesbian, gay, bisexual, transgender, queer, and (under the plus sign) other identities like intersex, pansexual, two-spirit, and asexual.

Even some of those words are umbrella terms themselves. While the word "gay" can identify men who love men, it can also be used as an umbrella term for anyone who identifies as not straight—someone who loves people who are the same gender. "Bisexual" is an umbrella term for the non-monosexual community, representing anyone who loves people of multiple genders, including people who identify as bisexual, pansexual, fluid, and so much more.

"Queer" is yet *another* umbrella term within the community. I personally use it as an identifying term because I love how it describes my sexuality, my gender, and my *politics* in opposition to normative society. Folks use the term "queer" for a lot of different reasons, especially if they feel a broad umbrella term like it helps them find a word for themselves when they might not squarely fit under other labels in the

LGBT acronym. Needless to say, we've got lots of umbrella terms embedded in the LGBTQ+ community. Umbrellas for umbrellas!

LET'S DECODE THE ACRONYM

Here are the different acronyms and what they stand for:

LGBT—Lesbian, Gay, Bisexual, Transgender

This version is most commonly and widely used. It's the acronym in its simplest form, and it's fine to use, but it's not the most inclusive version.

When you explain these letters to your little one, it can be helpful to start with the G because it's also an umbrella term like the acronym itself. Explain that someone who is homosexual or gay loves people who are their same gender. They are usually either a man who loves other men, or a woman who loves other women. Women who love women are also called lesbians, the L in LGBT. Being a gay or lesbian person is different from being straight or heterosexual, a person who only loves people who are a different gender than them. Someone who is straight is usually either a man who loves women or a woman who loves men.

Then we look at the B, which stands for bisexual. Someone who is bisexual loves people who are the same gender as them *and* people who are a different gender than them. Finally, we talk about the T, for transgender, a gender identity where a person does not identify with the gender they were assigned at birth.[22]

---

22 Folks who are nonbinary (or who love nonbinary people) might also identify as gay or lesbian instead of (or in addition to) identifying as bisexual. All of these terms have become a lot more fluid over the years,

GLBT—THE ORIGINAL ACRONYM

The original acronym for the LGBTQ+ community was GLBT. I see it pop up every once in a while, but the shift to "LGBT"—aka swapping the G and the L—was deliberate! Allegedly, LGBTQ+ rights activists switched the letters during the peak years of the HIV/AIDS crisis to recognize the humanitarian work lesbians had done as nurses and caregivers for their loved ones as they died from the epidemic.

LGBTQ—Lesbian, Gay, Bisexual, Transgender, Queer
This acronym is a lot more inclusive than LGBT because of the ways we use "queer" as an umbrella term with multifaceted definitions and loose boundaries.

LGBTQ+—Lesbian, Gay, Bisexual, Transgender, Queer, and more
This is my personal favorite and I use it the most in practice. It's a good mix of simple and inclusive without being too much of a mouthful. It's basically the same as LGBTQ, but the plus is an acknowledgment that there are many more identities that aren't included, and there's room for more.

LGBTQIA—Lesbian, Gay, Bisexual, Transgender, Queer, Intersex, Asexual
This version makes sure to include the intersex and asexual communities.

and different people use them in different ways! Basically, it's complicated, but don't worry about it too much!

Folks who are intersex are born with bodies that don't fit into what doctors would categorize, using the gender binary, as typical "boy" or "girl" bodies. Some intersex folks identify as trans or nonbinary, and some don't. Intersex identity is itself another umbrella that includes folks with a wide range of bodies, gender expressions, and identities.

Folks who identify as asexual do not feel sexual attraction. Asexuality exists on a spectrum and looks different for different people. (A common misconception is that asexual people don't have sex; that's not true and many of them do!) Under the umbrella term of asexual—often shortened to ace—are also folks who identify as aromantic, meaning they do not feel romantic attraction, an identity which, unsurprisingly, also exists on a spectrum. This is because everyone sits somewhere on the sexual and romantic attraction spectrums, even allosexual people (people who do experience sexual attraction). Intersex and asexual folks are as much a part of the community as any other letter!

EXPLAINING ASEXUALITY

Asexuality can be a tough identity to crack with kids, even though most prepubescent children are asexual themselves. Theoretically, it's an idea they should easily grasp, but it's a little tough to explain because it's a term that describes a specifically post-pubescent experience through an adult lens.

During an episode on asexuality for *Queer Kid Stuff*, YouTuber Elisa Hansen—who identifies as an asexual parent—and I discussed how kids might see grown-ups express their love for each other.

We talked about expressions of romantic love that adults might use with each other, like hugging and kissing. We differentiated romantic love between two grown-ups in a relationship from familial love, like between a parent and their child. By establishing these foundations in different types of relationships and types of love, we addressed how some grown-ups are asexual and might not want to express their romantic love for someone physically.

This conversation is also an opportunity to talk to young children about sex, consent, and body ownership. This is a slightly more advanced topic for elementary school kids, but if a kid is asking, don't be nervous to talk to them about it! And you can, again, address the idea of a spectrum. Like there is a gender spectrum, there is a spectrum of asexuality, too, and it's something that's separate from the gender of a person we love. It's another part of our sexuality.

Other Letters—P for Pansexual, 2S for Two-Spirit, Q for Questioning

You might see other versions of the acronym with these letters. Folks who are pansexual typically fall under the bisexual umbrella; the difference between bisexual and pansexual is nuanced, but essentially, pansexual folks typically don't care about gender at all—they love the person regardless of their gender identity.

Two-spirit (sometimes seen written as "2S") is specifically a pan-Indigenous gender identity that has existed for centuries (which you read about on page 148 in the nonbinary gender section). If a person is not from an Indigenous community, they shouldn't use this term for themselves.

Finally, sometimes you'll see a second *Q* in the acronym, which usually stands for folks who are questioning. Maybe they don't know what their sexuality is yet, are closeted, or they're exploring their sexuality. This one is really up for individual interpretation.

An Important Note on the *A*

You might have seen versions of the acronym that include *A* for ally. I haven't included that here because there is a very important distinction. While we love our allies and they are incredibly important, they are not themselves a *part* of the LGBTQ+ community in their own right. Allies can—and should—provide support and uplift the efforts of LGBTQ+ folks, but because they are not a part of the community itself, the thinking behind this is that they should not be included in the acronym that specifically describes the different identities within the LGBTQ+ community.

Gatekeeping can be harmful, but including *A* for ally in the LGBTQ+ acronym is different. The acronym is meant to describe a community of people who disrupt the normative world of straight cisgender folks with their identities simply by existing. Excluding allies from the acronym protects our community. This protection is different from the gatekeeping I've seen that happens in-community between people who think that some queer people are a part of the community and some aren't. For example, there are anti-trans people who are a part of the LGBTQ+ community who do not believe that transgender people should be included—they're called TERFs or "trans-exclusionary radical feminists." If you ever see someone or an organization use the acronym LGB that specifically excludes the *T* for trans, then you are probably dealing with TERFs! There are also folks who believe that intersex and asexual people shouldn't be "allowed," either, because some intersex and asexual people identify as heterosexual. But all of these people and identities still fall under the queer umbrella and they feel the effects of anti-queer discrimination. That kind of gatekeeping is toxic; anyone who feels *queer* and in direct opposition to the norm should be included in the acronym.

If a child in your life comes across a version of the LGBTQ+ acronym and wants to know what the letters mean, you can refer back to this book and approach these identities, as well as some of the different kinds of people who are considered a part of the LGBTQ+ community. There are lots more sexualities and gender identities that I didn't include here, and if you're interested, you can find a more robust list in the resources section in the back.

LET'S MAKE PRIDE FLAGS!

One way to help kids latch on to bigger vocabulary words and ideas around identity and sexuality is to introduce them to the beautiful spectrum of LGBTQ+ flags! You probably already know and love the famous rainbow flag originally created by Gilbert Baker in 1978 in San Francisco.

The rainbow flag as Baker originally designed it had eight colors, all of which stood for different queer concepts like sexuality and healing and the spirit, but eventually the colors were trimmed down and swapped out for manufacturing purposes. There are even more recently updated versions of the rainbow flag, like the Philadelphia version which added black and brown stripes to acknowledge everything that Black and Brown queer and trans people have done for the LGBTQ+ movement. And the newest flag, called the Progress Pride flag, which moves the black and brown stripes into a triangle on the left side of the flag and adds pink, blue, and white stripes to the triangle, to include the colors of the trans flag. There are also versions of this flag that include the yellow background and purple circle of the intersex flag. Gilbert Baker never trademarked the original flag, so he left us the gift of being able to update his original design. As our movement progresses, so do our symbols.

But there are tons of other flags, too, outside of the Rainbow, Philadelphia, and Progress flags! There are the original trans and intersex flags, the bisexual flag and the asexual flag and the lesbian flag and the nonbinary flag and countless others created by LGBTQ+ people over the years—mostly in the early aughts era of Tumblr—who wanted to celebrate their unique identities.

So grab your kid, some paper, a few crayons, and pick a flag, any flag! You'll be coloring for hours! You can even make your very own flags for your unique identities and have a conversation about different families and gender and love while you create together.

DIVING DEEPER INTO INTERSECTIONALITY

Let's build upon our discussions of intersectionality, social justice, and activism to dive deeper into topics like race, culture, ethnicity, class, disability and neurodivergency, religion, and more, as we think about how these parts of our identity might intersect with each other *and* everything we've learned so far about gender and sexuality. This will not be an in-depth exploration of topics like race, class, disability, etc. Each topic deserves its own full book, and many of these topics are not my lane, particularly as a white able-bodied person who grew up with access to wealth. But we *will* address how these other facets intersect with LGBTQ+ identity, so you can see more fully how to incorporate discussions of queerness into your anti-racism education with your kid, for example. There will be specific resources that you can look to, created by the voices (particularly queer voices) within those marginalized communities, so those folks can speak for themselves. Think of this chapter as an entry point for looking at these different facets of our identity from a specifically queer lens, and this book as a companion piece to the larger bodies of work around anti-racism, disability justice, and anti-capitalism, to name a few. The LGBTQ+ community is *incredibly* diverse within itself, and I hope this section helps you see the ways that these conversations about gender and sexuality intersect with every part of who we are and how we move through the world.

This section focuses less on how you can practically address these topics with kids and more on how you can re-center your conversations around them through a queer lens. But first, let's revisit our conversation on privilege, equality, equity, and justice.

EQUALITY, EQUITY, AND JUSTICE

Remember how we talked about fairness and unfairness in relation to privilege? And how privilege is like monkey bars, and how we can work together to imagine a brand-new jungle gym, "a place where everybody wins?" Let's talk more about how we can swing from our imaginary jungle gym and into the real world with a mission to rebalance the scales of social justice. In order to make that leap with kids, they first have to understand the differences between equality, equity, and justice. Here's a graphic from the Center for Story-based Strategy that truly blew my mind the first time I saw it.[23]

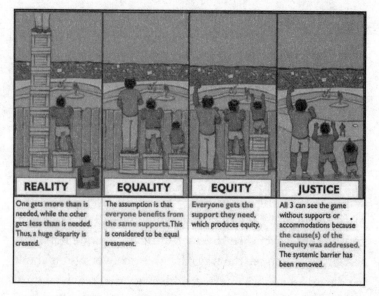

REALITY	EQUALITY	EQUITY	JUSTICE
One gets more than is needed, while the other gets less than is needed. Thus, a huge disparity is created.	The assumption is that everyone benefits from the same supports. This is considered to be equal treatment.	Everyone gets the support they need, which produces equity.	All 3 can see the game without supports or accommodations because the cause(s) of the inequity was addressed. The systemic barrier has been removed.

On the far left in "Reality," we can clearly see the *huge* advantage the person on the left has to see over the fence versus the other two people in the image. The person on the left has the most privilege, the person in the middle has enough privilege to see clearly, and the person on the right is actively disad-

23 https://www.storybasedstrategy.org/tools-and-resources.

vantaged and cannot see over the fence no matter what they do. "Equality" is where most grown-ups, particularly cisgender straight white people, get stuck in their understanding of justice. That person is probably exactly like the character on the left in the blue shirt who can see over the fence when everyone stands on equal-sized boxes even though the other two people are struggling. From their vantage point, it's easy to blame the person on the right's inability to see the fence on their height, rather than on the inequity of the boxes because all the boxes are technically "equal." But when we can step back and look at the full picture, we can immediately see injustice at work.

The next two panels of "Equity" and "Justice" show us what we can strive for beyond "Equality," to eradicate oppressive systems. Equality says that everyone deserves the exact same, but that approach does not take into account the privileges some are afforded over others—in this case, height! But when we look at equity, we see that resources are distributed *equitably,* or according to need. A methodological approach of *equity* is what could bring equality, whereas using the method of *equally* divvying up resources leads to more inequality, because it does not take the full circumstance and context into account.

The final panel of this series is that of "Justice"—it's also used interchangeably with "liberation" in some of their resources. In this image, the fence is taken down entirely, and there are no more barriers to access in anyone's way. That's what we are ultimately working toward.

Now, this viral graphic is not perfect. The metaphor of height difference between the characters reinforces a troubling implication that some people are inherently less than others. A graphic that had all the characters at the same height but where the ground sloped down unevenly would be a better metaphoric depiction of systemic oppression. The Center for Story-based Strategy also released a tool kit with the images for "Equality," "Equity," and "Justice/Liberation," but leaves a fourth box blank. This is where we get creative in our liberation, and where we can build a whole new jungle gym, "where everybody wins!"

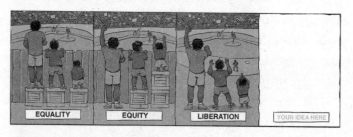

#THE4THBOX

MAKE YOUR OWN JUNGLE GYM

Pause here and get thinking with the young folks in your life; if you could completely rethink the world we live in, what would it look like? How would it be structured so the world isn't only equal or equitable or just? How can we make the world fit everyone's needs whether they are Black or Brown or Indigenous or white or trans or disabled? What does that world look like to you? What does the world look like if you let yourself reimagine it? How does reimagining it *with your kid* change it further? What does it look like? Grab your paper and markers and start an art project about it. Go wild!

RACE, CULTURE, AND ETHNICITY

I'm going to open this section up by restating that as a white person, I have *enormous* privilege because the world we live in was built for and continues to cater to white people like me. This section is where I step back and let others, particularly LGBTQ+ BIPOC (Black, Indigenous, People of Color) take the reins. It would be a disservice not to acknowledge the vital importance race plays in our identities and experience of the world, especially as a white person. There are incredible resources out there on bringing anti-racist and abolitionist education to young people, and I've included a number of them in the resource section of this book. Because here's the thing: if you aren't including LGBTQ+ BIPOC perspectives in your anti-racist work, then you're point-blank not doing it right.

What's even more important to get across here is for white and white-passing parents to understand that it is an absolute requirement that you talk to your kids about race. Doing the work of talking about gender and sexuality and bodies is simply not enough. White and white-passing people are inherently racist (and there are also people who are purposefully racist) because we were brought up in racism and have to unlearn it. In the same way that we are working to dismantle heteronormativity, we have to work to dismantle white supremacy. And while conversations around queerness versus conversations around race present different problems and oppressions that need to be reckoned with, the tactics and strategies for working against these oppressive systems are quite similar. Queer liberation works to dismantle white supremacy in the same way as anti-racism because both of these strategies uplift the most vulnerable people within those systems.

By putting anti-racism and queer liberation in conversation with each other, we are not uplifting BIPOC and queer and trans people separately from each other, but acknowledging that none of these identities are mutually exclusive. We can get specific about who is most marginalized and who is most vulnerable, and by lifting them up we can free every one of these systems—because if even one person isn't free, then we haven't done our jobs. That is the true work of queer liberation! And to get incredibly specific about who we are fighting for, we need to be talking about poor, disabled, Black trans women. These are the people we need to center in our work and in our advocacy and in our education. Practicing anti-racist queer liberation is how we let *all* kids be kids, whether they are Black or white or Latine or Asian or trans. In order to get there, we need to speak to young people about race *and* queerness.

The biggest hurdle, particularly for white parents, is the same one I see parents and educators get caught on when they approach LGBTQ+ topics. They are scared of the conversation itself. Folks get overwhelmed by big topics like gender, sexuality, and race because they don't know how to approach it "properly." But, as I hope you've learned so far, there really is no "proper" way to do it, as long as you have access to information and resources around these topics. You simply have to get out of your own way.

Megan Madison is a Black queer educator at the intersection of early childhood and anti-racism education and coauthor of the board book series First Conversations. In an interview with *Romper,* a well-regarded parenting and lifestyle blog, she discusses some of the pitfalls parents can find themselves in when talking about race and racism with young children:

1. thinking that you talk about race and racism once and then you're done (you're never done!)
2. waiting until a kid brings it up (which is usually too late)
3. striving for perfectionism and waiting until you know exactly the right thing to say (when you never will)
4. outsourcing these important conversations "by directing their kids to talk to 'this Black person I know,'" (this is not the way to be a good ally or comrade)
5. not talking about our own race and racial iden-tity (we need to be good models for young folks!)
6. feeling the need to sugarcoat it and gloss over the harder ideas and topics (this is where child-ism comes in, when we underestimate young folks)

These pitfalls are almost identical to the ones that come into play around conversations about gender, sexuality, queerness, and sex education. In the same way we got over our fears of talking about and centering queerness, we have to approach conversations about race with the same vigor and vulnerability, continuing to model curiosity for the young people in our lives. It's an incredibly similar approach, only a different topic to navigate. And guess what: if you've already talked about gender and sexuality with the kids in your lives, then you've already practiced the vulnerability and conversation tactics that you'll also use to address race! You're already flexing that muscle.

Parents and families of color are already talking about

race in their households, the same way queer and trans parents and families are talking about gender and sexuality. You can, too. In fact, it is *paramount* that white and white-passing adults talk about race. So flex those muscles again, take a look at the resource section in the back of this book for anti-racist books and shows and more, and go to town! In the same way you are recalibrating your environment to be less heterocentric, you can also work on making your environment less white-centered.

There are many ways to practice anti-racism, but one thing you can start to do—which we've already done around gender and sexuality—is look at your current picture book shelf, and think critically—through the lens of race this time—about the books and illustrations you are showing the children in your lives. You probably have a mix of classic and modern picture books. Maybe you'll pick up a classic picture book one day and notice for the first time that the characters in the background of a crowd scene are all white! (Look into Dr. Seuss's racist cartoons and think before you pick up your old copy of *The Cat in the Hat*; or consider Roald Dahl's well-documented antisemitism.) Think about whether you want to expose your child to works by these people, and how you can be critical of their work if you do introduce it, allowing young folks to make their own decisions about their content intake.

Don't let your nostalgia cloud your critical judgment. That's when you'll know that your sensitivity around race has begun to shift: when you can be critical of these texts and engage the young person you're reading to in that criticism by calling attention to it. Maybe they'll even notice before you!

CLASS AND CAPITALISM

Class, or socioeconomic status, is another important part of our identity that doesn't always get addressed with young people, even though many feel their grown-ups' financial strains in their everyday lives. My dad is a former fancy lawyer turned cool social justice lawyer, and my mom is a self-made entrepreneur turned senior executive, so growing up, I didn't want for much. But after graduating college and attempting to join the workforce, my own financial status took an abrupt nosedive. I tried to live in Brooklyn, on a $32,000 salary, as a receptionist and salesperson at a preschool and after-school program. I was grateful to have a job with a salary at all, and I will always have the privilege of my parents' economic status in emergency situations and greatly benefit from the education and opportunities they afforded me. Even so, this abrupt pivot in my personal finances showed me just how vital financial literacy and education is. And how my queer and trans identities have affected my ability to make money, particularly in a space as conservative and anti-queer as children's media.

Without a specific kind of financial education—particularly for folks in creative fields and in the arts sector—a lack of knowledge contributes to declining wealth in subsequent generations, even if older generations accumulated wealth. Look at the huge wealth gap between millennials and their parent baby boomers: According to a 2022 Bloomberg study, millennials hold only 4.6 percent of the wealth in America, or $5.19 trillion. In juxtaposition, *boomers hold 53.2 percent, or $59.96 trillion.* They are *ten times wealthier than millennials,* and twice as wealthy as Gen X. These financial inequities connect directly to not only our generational identities but also our gender, sexuality, race, etc. Many queer people are kept out of full-time job opportunities, face discrimination in the workplace including an inequitable pay gap, and so much more.

Kids see and feel socioeconomic differences in their everyday lives, from walking by their unhoused neighbors on their way to school, to not being able to get the fancy pair of sneakers like the rest of their friends, to working a part-time job or babysitting younger siblings after school instead of participating in extra curriculars, or completing home-work assignments.

This is something that educators should pay particular attention to, especially the unique socioeconomic disadvan-tages at play for LGBTQ+ families and families with multi-ple marginalized identities. When we consider the fight for an equal wage regardless of gender, we can look at two-mom households and understand that even if they have dual in-comes, there will probably be a large earning gap between their household and a straight household with a straight cisgender white man's salary. Or even for a same-sex white cis male household with *two* white cis male incomes. Ad-ditionally, workplace discrimination laws are not federally recognized as our politicians still struggle to pass the Equal-ity Act in Congress. As a result, many LGBTQ+ people are still not out at work and could be fired without those pro-tections in place. This has made things difficult particularly for LGBTQ+ educators and classroom teachers who do not feel safe being out in their schools. Even though it might seem like there has been significant progress in the fight for LGBTQ+ rights—and there has been!—there is still an in-credibly long way to go.

RAINBOW CAPITALISM

Rainbow capitalism—also called rainbow washing—has emerged over the last few years as LGBTQ+ people have become more visible to the corporate world as a way to build profits. Huge companies like Disney, Bank of America, AT&T, Pfizer, General Motors, even the CIA (?!) stick a rainbow flag on their social media accounts and merch. Rainbow washing gives the appearance that these huge corporations care about LGBTQ+ people, when in reality, they only care about their customers' *perception* that they support the LGBTQ+ movement. In fact, some of these companies actively use their power to fund anti-LGBTQ+ political campaigns.

Putting corporate dollars in the hands of actual queer and trans people is the way to go. For Pride 2022, for example, Skittles hired talented (and Instagram-popular) queer and trans graphic designers and illustrators to design their Pride Skittles wrappers. Even Target added compression binders and packing boxers (undies for trans guys!) to their 2022 Pride clothing line! These two examples are certainly steps in the right direction beyond slapping a rainbow on a Twitter avatar. Don't let corporate rainbow capitalism fool you, and do your best to support small queer and trans-owned businesses, *especially* during Pride Month.

Often, the people and families who need to have these conversations the most are not the ones who are most affected by these issues. Black and Brown parents generally talk to their kids about race, because it's something they know their kids will *feel* acutely in their everyday lives. The same goes for queer parents, particularly in same-sex parent households, whose kids encounter questions about their family's queerness in their everyday lives. The white and straight families who don't feel these oppressions are the ones who gloss over these important topics, to the detriment of marginalized families.

My parents rarely talked about money and wealth because it was something we had. My lack of understanding around my own privilege led to quite a reckoning in my midtwenties, and made my transition into my career incredibly difficult. What we can do now is what we've been doing all along: rewrite our learned understanding of the world. We can move forward with better and more diverse information to fix our broken systems that actively disenfranchise folks with marginalized identities who do not have access to generational wealth.

"WHAT DO YOU WANT TO BE WHEN YOU GROW UP?"

Here's where I'm gonna go off on a little anti-capitalist rant, because even though you might not realize it, every single thing in our American society is underpinned by capitalist values, and that includes the lessons we impart to young people. One of the first questions we ask young children is "what do you want to be when you grow up?" This question imagines a child's future in the same way an adult might assume that a child will grow up to be straight and cisgender. In this case, I challenge your assumption that children dream of labor. Why are young folks only taught to yearn to be useful to our economy? Why aren't they encouraged to pursue their passions and interests and live in the moment and *enjoy their childhood,* above all else? This is capitalism at work on children. Why do we only put A's and A+'s on our refrigerators instead of B's and C's? Why do we encourage kids to do community service projects only so they'll have something that will look good on their college applications?

Why is getting into a "good kindergarten" akin to getting into an Ivy League university? And what makes one school or university better than another outside of wealth hoarding, gatekeeping, and scandal-riddled yet somehow un-besmirched reputations? Why are parents so hell-bent on their children growing up to be "successful," and why can't we simply want our kids to grow up and be *happy*? So how about the next time you ask a child, "What do you want to *be* when you grow up?" try shifting just slightly to ask, "What are some things that make you *happy*?"

Anti-capitalist parenting doesn't always look like having specific conversations with your children. It can look like deciding to send them to a public school instead of a private school; it can look like teaching them about financial literacy through their allowance; it can look like modeling how to redistribute wealth to nonprofit organizations and local mutual aid funds, investing in small businesses, and divesting from huge for-profit companies like Amazon that employ unsafe and unfair labor practices in their warehouses. It can look like celebrating that participation trophy like it was first-place gold, and it can look like asking, "What makes you happy?" instead of "What do you want to be when you grow up?" It is not possible to live 100 percent ethically under capitalism, but we can teach kids how to navigate the existing system, make informed choices about their finances, and maybe even work toward changing the system themselves one day.

DISABILITY AND NEURODIVERSITY

There is an enormous correlation between people who are neurodivergent and also identify as LGBTQ+, particularly trans and/or nonbinary people. Dr. Diane Ehrensaft coined the term "Double Helix Rainbow Kids" to describe children who are on both the autism and gender spectrums.[24] Autistic people are two to three times more likely to identify as LGBTQ+ than their neurotypical peers! As someone who worked through a neurodivergent diagnosis in their late twenties, discovered mostly through TikTok, I can personally attest to the fact that neurodivergence, particularly

---

24 Okay, so technically everyone is on the gender spectrum, but here I'm specifically talking about trans, nonbinary, and gender non-conforming kiddos!

ADHD and autism, are underdiagnosed, especially in AFAB (remember, that's assigned female at birth) folks.

But the neurodivergent community (where we recognize that not only are our bodies diverse, but our brains are as well) is only one part of the vast movement of disability justice. Disability justice includes folks with mental illnesses; physically disabled people; people who are deaf or hard of hearing; people who are visually impaired or legally blind; folks with chronic pain and chronic illnesses; and developmentally, cognitively, and intellectually disabled people— and there are queer people across all of those categories! And a lot of them are kids.

We talk about marriage equality within the LGBTQ+ movement and how we achieved the right to same-sex marriage through *Obergefell v. Hodges* in 2015, but what we frequently gloss over is the fact that true marriage equality has not yet been achieved in the United States. This is because disabled people cannot legally get married without losing their vital and sometimes lifesaving disability income.

Disability status is the only marginalized identity that can happen to *anyone* at any point in their lives. But it's also something many adults are scared to talk about with kids, not unlike the fears that exist around conversations about gender, sexuality, bodies, and race (see a pattern emerging?). Disabled people get the same kinds of questions about their bodies as transgender people. Some disabled people are comfortable answering questions about their bodies, but most don't want to talk to strangers on the street about traumatic accidents that changed their lives or complex diagnoses that are very personal. We have to approach disability with the same vulnerability, care, empathy, and openness we've learned about when approaching gender, bodies, and race.

Like we are making race and gender and sexuality more visible to kids, make sure that the resources you are using and engaging with are inclusive of disabled people and their stories, that you work to recognize common ableist language and stigmas, and that you are talking consciously about those disabilities instead of skating over them.

MENTAL HEALTH

Mental health is an incredibly important topic that is being talked about more in mainstream discourses. Let's go back to some of those stats we covered when we talked about the state of LGBTQ+ youth: according to a survey conducted by The Trevor Project on the effects of COVID-19 on LGBTQ+ youth, nearly half of LGBTQ+ youths stated that COVID-19 impacted their ability to express their sexual orientation, and nearly 60 percent of transgender and nonbinary youth said the pandemic impacted their ability to express their gender identity.[25] The COVID-19 pandemic forced so many LGBTQ+ kids and young folks into spaces and situations where they were not safe to live as their authentic selves, wreaking absolute havoc on their mental health. Imagine being stuck in a house without being able to leave where the people around you called you by the wrong name, used the wrong pronouns, and you couldn't even wear clothes that made you feel good because you were scared that they'd kick you out, or disown you simply for being who you are.

The year 2020 in particular changed the narratives around mental health because let's face it: being trapped at

---

25 https://www.thetrevorproject.org/trvr_press/new-research -underscores-mental-health-disparities-faced-by-diverse-lgbtq-youth -amid-covid-19-beyond/.

home on and off for more than a year was not good for our brains, especially for kids and even more so for LGBTQ+ young folks. I've dealt with bouts of depression and anxiety in my life, am a survivor of sexual assault, and am married to a person with diagnosed anxiety and depression. The online abuse I went through when I started *Queer Kid Stuff* was traumatic and has had a lasting impact on my mental health. Being in therapy on and off throughout the years has helped me work through and process my emotions and reactions to what has happened in my life, alongside a recent mindfulness practice of weekly yoga and daily(ish) meditation and exercise. All this paired with strong boundaries that help separate my work from my life. I think I'm in a relatively stable state in my current mental health, but it's something that necessitates constant work.

There are many things that might impact an LGBTQ+ person's mental health because of their identity, but we should be talking about mental health and taking care of it no matter who we are or what our identity is, in order to destigmatize mental health and teach young people to prioritize their well-being.

Queer and trans people grow up in a society that tells us our identities are not acceptable. Many of us grow up with parents who don't understand, in spaces that are not safe for us. (Go you for actively working to *understand* and *be safe* for queer and trans kids!) For many queer and trans people, there is a delay of sorts that happens in our lives. Since I didn't come out until I was in college, I wasn't living as my authentic self all through my teen years. The milestones teens typically hit—including dating and having crushes and other healthy social development—don't happen on the same timelines as most straight folks. I didn't start dating queerly until my junior year of college! But the times are, of course, a-changin' and LGBTQ+ folks are coming out younger and younger. According to a 2021 Gallup survey, "one in every six Gen Z respondent identifies as queer or trans compared to one in every ten Millennials." So progress is surely being made. Queer and trans young people are coming out way younger than we used to because they have greater access to LGBTQ+ representation and education, which is awesome! But that doesn't mean this work isn't incredibly necessary. We need to introduce all of these topics early and consistently in order to combat negative mental health in young folks, especially LGBTQ+ young folks. That's exactly the work of this book!

It's important to learn about and understand the different techniques that can help *you* manage your mental health, but there are also ways we can do this with our kids, too! Kids can and *should* have access to therapy, especially if they are going through big life changes. Continuing to emphasize and teach your kid to practice body kindness and self-care is an incredible tool they can use throughout their lives. And meditation and yoga practices for kids are becoming more and more prevalent. Mindfulness is also an excellent way to introduce tools and techniques to young kids that will help them learn to regulate their emotions and mental health. There are plenty of mindfulness apps nowadays with programs for children and lots of kid-friendly yoga options. If you're looking for a place to start, first ask yourself how you practice mindfulness in your own life and get creative in how you can not only model your practice to the kids, but also bring them into your practice to turn mental health into a family ritual.

RELIGION

The religious and queer communities have had quite a lot of conflict, to say the least, but that doesn't mean that there aren't LGBTQ+ people of every faith, no matter how accepting the traditional teachings are. There are LGBTQ+ Jews and LGBTQ+ Muslims, and LGBTQ+ Christians and Buddhists and Quakers, but not all of these religions and faiths have been kind to LGBTQ+ people. Organized religions have caused a lot of pain for LGBTQ+ people, but when they are inclusive and welcoming, they can also be havens.

Faith is complex in the queer community, especially for those who grew up in hostile religious environments. Some queer adults went through the horrific torture of conversion therapy at the hands of their church and their biological family. Every queer and trans person processes such trauma at their own pace and level, and some work to find their own spirituality and faith that makes sense for their lives outside of the religions they grew up in—some become rabbis and ministers; others are atheist and agnostic. I grew up and still identify as a Reform Jew, but I've also found spiritual fulfillment through astrology and light mysticism. Many queer and trans folks have learned to take their spirituality and faith into their own hands outside the confines of organized religion to find something that works for their lives and understanding of identity and the world.

So if you're sending your kids to Hebrew school or Bible study, make sure you are in a religious environment that isn't only accepting but also openly welcome to LGBTQ+ families. Work with your kids to nuance their understanding of faith. Give them space to connect with their cultural heritage and history—which can be inextricably tied to religion—and let them know that they can navigate their faith for themselves, too!

CLIMATE CHANGE AND NATIVE JUSTICE

The climate justice movement addresses issues every single person feels no matter their identities or marginalizations, because our Earth is sick, which affects all living creatures, including humans, even queer humans! If you care about the kids in your life and their future happiness, then you need to care about climate justice and how we can heal our sick planet. And we need to talk about how climate change affects us all because intersectionality is incredibly relevant when we talk about how climate change impacts different marginalized communities, particularly the queer and trans communities that have less access to basic necessities during climate disasters.

Before getting into what you typically might think of as climate justice, I want to emphasize that a huge part of climate justice is Native justice. Indigenous and Native peoples are the original stewards of Turtle Island[26] (aka North America) before European colonizers committed widespread genocide of Native peoples across the Western Hemisphere, stole Native land through force and illegally violated treaties, murdered thousands of Native children in so-called residential assimilationist boarding schools where we are still unearthing mass burial sites, and destroyed their sacred land and water for capitalistic profiteering with no regard for the good of our planet. I know that's a lot to take in, but

26 Turtle Island is the term commonly used by Native peoples to refer to North America. It comes from a common creation story from Native American folklore, particularly from Lenape and Iroquois oral storytelling traditions.

the atrocities Native peoples have suffered at the hands of white colonizers is unfathomable. We have desecrated Native peoples and their culture and in tandem taken our Earth for granted. European colonization has detrimentally impacted Native peoples, our planet, and even serve as the origin for many of the rigid ideas around sexuality and gender that we are dismantling in this book!

Climate justice (and anti-racism work *and* queer liberation, too!) is Native justice: practicing land acknowledgments to educate ourselves on Native land stewardship, learning about the Land Back movement and giving lands back to Indigenous peoples, and fighting against the oil pipelines that leak into Indigenous lands and destroy agriculture and sacred water supplies. We can work together to decolonize our society from all forms of oppression. We also need to work within the queer community to recognize indigiqueer[27] and two-spirit identities as a part of our queer liberation. Justice for Native communities and our Earth are vital for the continued survival of every single human on our planet regardless of age, gender, sexuality, race, and disability.

A LAND ACKNOWLEDGMENT FOR THIS BOOK!

This book was written on stolen land of the Wabanaki Confederacy currently comprised of the Penobscot, Passamaquoddy, Maliseet, and Micmac tribes. It was edited on the island of Mannahatta

---

27 A term coined by two-spirit Native scholar and writer Joshua Whitehead that describes folks at the intersections of queerness and indigineity.

on the ancestral land of the Lenape peoples. It was printed in Virginia. All of this took place on Turtle Island, a land that was stolen and settled by European colonizers who committed genocide against the land's stewards and Native peoples.

I would also like to add a pledge to my land acknowledgments because mere acknowledgment isn't enough. I (Lindz) pledge to uplift indigiqueer and two-spirit voices through my work as a queer and trans activist and pay monthly reparations to the Wabanaki Confederacy as a part of my Land Back practice.

That's an example of a land acknowledgment with a pledge of action. If you want to learn about the Native peoples whose land you occupy, you can use the map on https://native-land.ca to start your journey.

Outside of Native justice, climate change disproportionately affects other marginalized communities, particularly those who do not have access to stable housing when temperatures and water levels are on the rise alongside extreme weather conditions. Individually, we can work to reduce our waste through composting, recycling, and reducing our use of nonreusable plastics; we can use public transportation and eco-friendly electric cars, eat less red meat, and try to curb our individual contributions to climate change; but, ultimately, the perpetrators of climate change are large profit-driven corporations that care far more about their bottom line than the destruction of our planet.

So talk to your kid about climate change in the same breath as Native justice and decolonization. Show them how to recycle bottles and plastics. Teach them how to sew on their own buttons so they can repair their clothes instead of tossing them in the trash and buying something new. Take them to a nearby community beach pickup or start one yourselves! Find awesome local organizations to donate lightly used coats and hats and gloves in the winter. There are *lots* of ways you can teach your kids about climate justice and practice sustainability. Show them how we can work as individuals to stay educated and model your own advocacy, pushing for green legislation from our lawmakers and divesting from corrupt organizations that are killing our planet. Let's teach the next generation to treat our planet and our land's Native peoples with respect!

FOCUSING YOUR ACTIVISM

Social justice covers a *lot* of topics and inequities. We're not just talking about queer liberation but also disability justice, racial equality, Native justice, climate change, reproductive justice, animal rights, abolition, economic justice and fighting for unhoused peoples, feminism, reproductive rights, and a whole lot more. While it is important to understand all of these issues, we are still human and humans have limits! We cannot always be fully engaged activists in every movement; it's simply not physically possible. But we don't have to be—nor should we be—on the front lines of every movement in order to be an effective activist. At the beginning of your journey as an activist and on your path to figuring out what that looks like for you and your family, you need to find your focus.

Your focus can be fluid. You do not have to pick one movement and only ever concentrate on that activism. Finding your activist *home* is all about prioritizing what you are most passionate about, where your voice and body and work are going to be most effective, and what role you want to take within that movement. While I have multiple marginalized identities, I found early on that the identity that I struggled with the most was being a part of the LGBTQ+ community, and it felt natural for that to be my primary focus. From there, I winnowed that down even further to focus specifically on queerness and children's media and storytelling. But like I said, that doesn't mean you leave other movements behind, at all. While most of my dedicated labor is in queer stuff for kids, I also work to stay activated in other justice movements as best I can.

One way to stay activated in other justice movements is by diversifying your feeds, staying up-to-date on current news and information, and sharing resources so you can keep your communities informed. And you can always look at these movements in communication and coalition with each other. Constantly ask yourself, "How can I practice active anti-racism and uplift Black trans women in my own work as an activist? How can I be an ally to folks fighting for disability justice, especially those who are queer and/or trans?" Your focus will likely feel incredibly personal. Find where you are connected to injustice and discover what lights your fire and keeps you going in this work. Ask your kid what social justice movement really gets them going. How can you help them use that activism as a lens to engage with other social justice movements?

A TRANS PERSPECTIVE ON
REPRODUCTIVE RIGHTS

An example of bringing my queer and trans perspective to a movement is in reproductive rights! It might not *seem* like a relevant topic for kids, but families come together in so many different ways, and sometimes, abortion is a part of that story. If we are talking to kids about reproduction (like we did way back in toddlerhood!), we should also be talking to them about abortion and reproductive rights. If you don't know where to start, the picture book *What's an Abortion, Anyway?* is a perfect resource for introducing kids to the topic of abortion. But we don't have to talk about abortion and reproductive rights in isolation from queerness and transness for two reasons: (1) Abortion is also a trans issue! Some nonbinary and transmasculine people have uteruses, which means they also get abortions! And (2) the heart of the matter is bodily autonomy (wait a second, we've already been talking to kids about that!).

Trans rights and reproductive rights are about bodily autonomy and access to healthcare. I'm not picking one over the other. I'm allowing my expertise in one to inform how I interact with another to build *coalition*. I know so many trans people who get their hormones from Planned Parenthood! These two rights movements have their core issues in common! What I hope is becoming clearer as you move through this section is that, in many ways, we are all fighting the same monster. While movements that fight for reproductive rights and trans rights might have different goals and are coming from different experiences, they are both fighting for control over the decisions we can make about our bodies. The same can be said for the Black Lives Matter movement and climate justice. We are all working toward liberation around our bodies and access to resources. I think the overarching ubiquity of queerness across all of these sectors can unlock a coalition of justice movements that we can and *should* take part in alongside our children.

THERE'S NO ONE WAY TO BE AN ACTIVIST

While you and your family find your foothold within activism, you'll notice that activism isn't only one thing—it takes many different forms and isn't limited to protesting and organizing. Activism is about causing disruption, and that can happen on the street, within established industries, through art, on social media—virtually anywhere and in any way.

Maybe when you put down this book, you'll share something you learned from it on social media and recommend it or loan it to a friend to read. That's participating in activism! When you talk to your kids about gender and pronouns and sexuality and privilege and consent, that's participating in activism! Writing this book is a part of my activism! Going into a library and singing, "It's okay to be gay," to a roomful of families is activism! When you fly a rainbow flag in your yard, that's activism! When you put a Black Lives Matter sign in the children's section of your library or in your school's hallway, that's activism! Art is activism! Marching is activism! Organizing is activism! These things can all be activism when they are connected to a disruptive mission. We can all contribute differently to change-making efforts by disrupting our immediate spaces and using our strengths and skill sets and privileges to change oppressive systems and shift the culture.

Now that your kid is school age, they can get involved as activists and take different direct actions to make a difference. That's not to say you can't take your three-year-old to a protest, you for sure can! But when they're school age, they are starting to understand most of what's going on around them, *why* they are there, and *what* they are doing in the first place. So yes, you can and *should* take your kid to protests, but you can also volunteer with a local organization as a family or class. You can hold a bake sale or set up a lemonade stand to raise money. You can take them with you to local city council and school board meetings to speak up about issues in your community. Get creative!

ALLYSHIP VS. COMRADERY

A huge and incredibly important component of your activism is going to be comradery and allyship. Along your journey, you will likely participate in justice movements as someone *supporting* a marginalized community toward their liberation. You'll be on the sidelines cheering these movements along instead of standing in the center of them. That's what it means to be an ally or *comrade*. I first heard the term "comrade"[28] at an educators' conference in Brooklyn where Brittany Packnett Cunningham, a prominent Black activist on the front lines of the Black Lives Matter movement, spoke to NYC-based teachers and school administrators interested in social justice education. She called for comradery as an alternative to allyship.

You're probably already familiar with allyship. I'm sure you've seen countless "How to Be a Good Ally" articles and listicles and Instagram infographics that tell you how to educate yourself, be more inclusive, and "put yourself in someone else's shoes." To add to that, an ally is also someone who supports people who are different from them. There are three components to being a good ally:

1.   We must respect others and their identities,
2.   we must listen to others who have identities that are different from our own, and
3.   we must be open to learning from others.

Allyship is about redistributing the power you have from your privilege to people who are more marginalized than you. Straight people can be allies to queer people, and cisgender people can be allies to transgender people, and white people can be allies to Black and Brown people—the list goes on and on. That's all fine and good, and it *is* important to talk about allyship and what it means to be an ally, but it is not an end point or an achievement. It is something to consistently aspire to.

---

28 Maybe you associate the term "comrade" with communism and the former Soviet Union, but it actually originated as a term between socialists in the French Revolution before Marxists adopted it in their labor-organizing practices. Cold War–era pop culture is largely to blame for its associations with communism!

If you're reading this book, you've likely categorized yourself as an ally at some point. But here's where we have to ask ourselves what have we done to be an *active* ally to that community, outside of simply pronouncing ourselves as one. Allyship is about being supportive of marginalized people and communities, yes, but it's more than that.

When discussing allyship with kids, you can talk about the importance of listening, learning, and respecting with others. It's the walk-a-day-in-someone-else's-shoes thing. You have to accept that your experience isn't the same as others, and that is an *incredibly* important lesson for kids to learn! Children's theater has been called a "gymnasium for empathy,"[29] and there is neurologically based research that shows how live theater and storytelling help children develop their capacity for empathy. Stories, books, theater, shows, and movies help us understand experiences outside of our own.

When we accept this seemingly simple idea, we open ourselves up to listen to others' stories and experiences. That's where we can *learn*—about other people, the issues that impact their lives, their joys and their struggles. We can learn firsthand what they want and what they need. Listening to and learning from others is what helps us develop our capacity for empathy, because empathy is not something we are born with; it's something that must be taught and exercised until it becomes second-nature muscle memory.

The question here is what does "good allyship" *do*? If we

29 Gunderson, Lauren. "How Theater for Young People Could Save the World," *HuffPost*, accessed January 10, 2023, https://www.huffpost.com/entry/world-theater-for-children-and-young-people-day_b_1343408.

see all of these rigid and oppressive systems that enact harm on marginalized people, including and beyond the queer community, then we should be trying to fix those systems and help those oppressed peoples. But does allyship do that? Maybe good allyship makes things a bit more comfortable for marginalized people, but that's still working within these oppressive systems. We are trying to dismantle, reimagine, and rebuild, and good allyship won't get us there. That's where comradery comes in.

The difference between allyship and comradery is in the way you actively put your privilege on the line to help marginalized folks. Being a comrade is about a whole lot more than proclaiming yourself an "ally," or putting a "safe space" sticker on your water bottle or laptop. Comradery goes beyond good or even *best* allyship—the bare minimum. It's the first step on the way to comradery because allyship alone is not how we make true lasting change.

It's the difference between baking cupcakes for your child's school bake sale to raise funds for a nonprofit versus working reparations and mutual aid donations into your monthly budget to consistently redistribute a small portion of your wealth to marginalized peoples in your communities (while the billionaires who hoard 80 percent of the world's wealth double their net worth lounging on their yachts). It's the difference between a white person *attending* a protest versus a white person *physically putting their body* between a police officer and a Black protestor at a Black Lives Matter protest. The difference is specific and physical and impactful. Allyship is well meaning but passive; comradery is hard and uncomfortable and even scary, but is what actively moves us toward true systemic change, through disruption. Think of allyship as a stepping stone toward comradery. We have to get to allyship first, but we have to push past our comfort zone toward comradery.

We have to get through our fear and discomfort because marginalized people already occupy that space. We confront this danger zone in our daily lives. That is true for all marginalized people. I get misgendered on an almost daily basis. My wife and I get addressed as "ladies" at restaurants. I get "ma'am"-ed by customer service agents on the phone. People assume that I use she/her pronouns *all the time*. It is exhausting. I've given up on correcting people because it turns into a *thing* every single time, and I have to continually shoulder that emotional burden over and over and over again, first in the misgendering itself and then again in the education. Because of this, I am almost always in a state of discomfort around strangers, when I'm not in an explicitly queer space or around close friends and chosen family. My wife and I are usually pretty comfortable holding hands as we walk down the street, but we both have strong instincts to drop them if we see someone nearby in a MAGA hat because of the anti-queer beliefs it historically implies. We visited my grandparents in Arizona one holiday season, and I asked my wife not to kiss me at a movie theater because I didn't feel safe in what I felt was a conservative space.

So how do you shift from allyship to comradery? If you are in a position of privilege, you can start by clearing a path and paving the way. Stretch that privilege to its fullest extent and further your mission by bringing your community along with you. For me, I know that my whiteness has given me incredible opportunities and access. I have enough privilege so that I can survive and make a living while I continue forward in this incredibly difficult work, where I'm pushing against gatekeepers to advocate for LGBTQ+ stories and characters in mainstream children's media. There are so few people who do this work alongside me in the mainstream children's media space because it's incredibly difficult and mostly thankless. I know that I would not be able to do what I do without my whiteness, plain and simple. Using my whiteness to get into spaces where I can obtain the power to uplift others is how I grapple with this. And you'll have to figure this part out for yourself wherever your privileges lie, too.

Comradery is so much more than allyship. It's the work that will disrupt our oppressive systems, and families and kids can be a part of that process in the spaces they occupy. It might feel scary to think about within your family. If you're nervous about putting yourself out there as a comrade, how can you begin to think about talking to your family and even kids about comradery? Try to remind yourself that kids from BIPOC and otherwise marginalized families and with marginalized identities face the same dangers as adults in these identities and are even more vulnerable in many ways. It doesn't matter their age, a Black child is still Black, a trans child is still trans, and society still treats them accordingly.

I'm not suggesting that a white child should stand in between a cop and a Black person at a protest because that is first of all, obviously dangerous, and second, it's not where their privilege can be used to be the most helpful. You can be a comrade to your child and the childism they face by letting them know they can come to you and you will *actively* support them by, for example, helping them voice their discomfort with something their teacher said to them in class. You can talk to your kids about being an upstander when they see someone in their class getting bullied, too. You and your family can become comrades in ways that are relevant to your lives. Maybe you're a white or white-passing person whose workplace has unethical labor practices that have a greater impact on your colleagues of color. Assess the situation and see what you can actively do that can change the systemic problem you are diagnosing. Your whiteness makes you far less vulnerable to losing your job than your colleagues of color. Maybe your comradery becomes advocating for better working conditions and eventually leading an effort to form a labor union at your company that will benefit everyone and gives your BIPOC colleagues a seat at the negotiating table!

As always, remember to take care of yourself throughout your activism. You are only one person. I constantly ask myself if I am doing enough in comradery with BIPOC, disabled folks, unhoused people, and so many more who have less privilege than I do. In many ways, I'm not doing enough and I will never be able to do enough, and that's part of the discomfort I have to sit with. But those thoughts in themselves are also incredibly flawed because there is no such thing as perfection in this work. Don't get caught up in the tendency to overwork yourself—that's the capitalistic attitude that fuels hustle culture and leads to burnout. I used to burn out constantly! We cannot be good advocates or allies or comrades if we burn out too quickly—it's not sustainable and it's exactly what these oppressive systems want from us in the first place. They want us to *fail*! Do the work, but pay attention to your needs, too. As Rabbi Tarfon—one of the great Jewish sages of history—says, "It is not your responsibility to finish the work [of perfecting the world], but you are not free to desist from it either."

You do the work while you're alive on this earth, knowing you'll have to leave it unfinished when you're gone. You prepare your kids and the next generation to pick up the work after you. *That's* the whole point of this book and what we are building toward together.

GETTING COMFORTABLE WITH DISCOMFORT

If you're not a little bit uncomfortable in your activism, then it might be time to more closely examine *how* you approach your activism. This is where things get hard. Where they get messy and chaotic and nuanced. We are all humans in this world, and that means that we are inevitably going to make mistakes and hurt people along the way whether it's intentional or not.

Impact always takes precedent over intent. Maybe you have the best of intentions at heart. But you can't take back harm you've done to someone. Even though the harm I'm talking about is mostly felt internally, we can still think about it physically. Imagine if calling someone a derogatory slur—this is an extreme example—physically broke their arm. You can't undo breaking someone's arm even if you didn't intend to break it. So what do you do when you realize your impact wasn't what you intended?

You apologize. You make a *good* apology where you take accountability for your actions, call out the harm you caused, explain why it was harmful, and vow to do better next time. The damage has already been done so take accountability and move on. It's *really* important to practice how to give a good apology yourself so you can teach and model how to give one to your kids. You *will* inevitably make mistakes, so practice and prepare yourself to deal with their consequences with grace, vulnerability, and determination to not do that same harm again.

In the heyday of Facebook groups, I observed digital social justice spaces that would inevitably implode on themselves. Someone would post or comment something ignorant. Then someone else in the group would call them out and the original poster/commenter would get defensive and double down. Then moderators wouldn't know how to handle the situation because of their own biases, and other voices would chime in with other instances of racist/anti-trans/anti-gay altercations in the group. That would over-whelm the space before someone made an alternate offshoot group. The original group would either fester in its lack of ability to see its own faults and slowly die out as more and more people left the toxicity of that space, or it would implode completely and get deleted. I did not just see this happen once, I saw it happen *many times*. There are many reasons why this occurs in social justice–oriented spaces, but I think a huge reason why is because, particularly in digi-tal social spaces where nuance can easily get lost, we don't know how to be comfortable with being uncomfortable.

We—and I'm talking to white people here in particular—have to know when to use our voices to support and advo-cate, and understand when it is not our place or our lane. We have to know when to stand up *and* when to step back. This is crucial and it's always an ongoing internal (and sometimes external) conversation. No matter what I do in my work as a queer and trans activist, I will always be a white person. That means that my work as a writer, performer, media-maker, and figurehead of an organization will always be centered around my whiteness. I ask myself *constantly* if I should be doing the work I'm doing and if I'm the right person for this work. I ask myself what can I be doing to actively de-center myself and my whiteness in my work and use the power I can leverage with my whiteness in order to open the door for queer and trans people of color and others who are more marginalized than I am.

I wonder if there will be a time when I've forged enough of a path to be able to pass the baton on to others who are better suited to be at the front of this movement. I don't want to do this work alone forever and, furthermore, I *shouldn't* do this work alone forever and take up space I could pass off to someone else. This is an ongoing conversation I will probably *always* have with myself and within my work. This push and pull is a huge part of the discomfort. There is no escaping this particular inner turmoil, so you have to get comfortable. Constantly learn from and seek out opportunities, diversify your social media feeds, and find ways to support queer and trans people with perspectives outside your own. Model this to the kids in your life. Good comradery is uncomfortable and we have to settle into that discomfort if we are going to make real, true, lasting systemic change. And that is true activism!

UPSTANDERS VS. BYSTANDERS

I would be remiss if I got through this entire book without talking about bullying. While there are plenty of grown-ups who are bullies, the issue comes up the most with young kids. When they enter upper elementary school and into middle school, some kids—for whatever reason—can be very mean. For those who aren't the bullies but also aren't the target, it's easy to either fade into the background or climb onto the bandwagon.

Or, your child can practice being a comrade at school by being an upstander, as opposed to a bystander who sits on the sidelines. Standing up for someone else is no easy task. It takes a great deal of courage to put yourself on the line, but this is how we stop bullying. Talking to the bullies about changing their ways is not how we get there—the truth is that they won't listen. What stops bullying in the moment is intervention from upstanders.

I wasn't expressly bullied as a kid. There were definitely moments when kids were mean and I never quite fit in, or I hung out with the wrong people, but I do vividly remember moments when I stayed silent. When I saw someone get bullied, I shrunk into myself instead of doing the brave thing and standing up for that person. I went to a hoity-toity all-girls school for elementary school, in the land of the *Gossip Girl* kids who have their own drivers at the age of five and everything else that is inherited by the obscenely generationally wealthy. My family is not like that; I stood out because I was the *downtown kid*. I wanted so badly to fit in, even though I didn't, but I didn't want people to think I was weirder than they already did, so I didn't stick my nose out, either.

There was one girl who was bullied particularly badly in my grade. A whole group of popular girls would sit down at a table, and when this girl would try to sit down in an empty seat next to them, the entire group would get up and move to another table. I didn't say anything. It got so bad that the teachers had to make a rule that you weren't allowed to switch tables once you put your tray down. I think about that girl a lot because I knew I could say something about it, but I didn't want to put myself in the line of fire.

When I presented as more feminine as a tween and teen, I was constantly harassed by men on the streets of Manhattan. When I started to present authentically and more androgynously and masculine, the street harassment stopped. This is my masculine privilege. I remember walking down the street in Williamsburg at night in my midtwenties on the way to the subway from a bar, and I saw a pair of women in dresses and heels walk down the street and pass a group of men who whistled, catcalled, and started to follow them. The women looked visibly uncomfortable and asked the men to stop following them, but they didn't stop. I was right behind the men, and I knew I had to do something or they would keep following the women, and that could end with the men sexually assaulting the women. I got up my courage and spoke up, "They told you to stop, leave them alone." The men gave me a bewildered look, but they stopped in their tracks. They got in their last word before they moved in a different direction. I passed the girls who looked scared. I gave them a quick nod, asked if they were okay, then went on my way, and the women continued on theirs.

That moment wasn't easy for me, but it was the bare minimum I could do to use my masculine privilege to interrupt a dangerous situation. I wasn't thinking about myself in that moment; I was thinking about the potential danger those girls were in. There's no need to pat myself on the back for the bare minimum that I did, but I helped people who needed someone on their side with more power than them.

In these situations, remind your child that they have the power to change someone's circumstances. They can help someone who is in trouble, and they'll feel *good* afterward! Comradery is rewarding. Teach young kids to do the courageous thing and stand up for others when they have power that could significantly change the outcome, and be sure to model that behavior for them.

You can show kids how to be allies, comrades, and upstanders by being one yourself. You can talk about these topics over and over, but most kids learn best from example, especially when they reach kindergarten and beyond. So get involved! Push yourself so you can push them. Bring them along with you to marches and protests. Point out allyship and comradery in media. Try to make allyship and comradery visible for young people in your example and in others you admire.

Get involved with local nonprofit organizations and maybe even come up with a project of your own to help your community. Or talk to your family about how you want to spend some extra money in your budget, and work as a family to decide on different mutual aid funds to donate to every month. Maybe go through your children's old clothes with them and talk about food and clothing drives and donations. Talk to your kid's school or community center about doing a community art project like a mural with a meaningful message. Organize a day of action with your neighbors to petition your local government! There is so much work to do out there, and all you have to do is figure out how you want to start doing it together.

INTRODUCING LGBTQ+ HISTORY TO YOUR KID

Did you know that October in America is LGBTQ+ History Month? Queer history is often cast aside or made fully invisible from most school history classes, not unlike histories of other marginalized groups. Despite what your textbooks might tell you, queer people have been around for pretty much all of recorded history, but you might have to actively seek it out beyond the classroom. The following section—the tip of the iceberg—dives into some LGBTQ+ history. Take this as an overview and think about the ways you can unearth queer history for yourself and the young folks in your

life so they can see the origins of the modern queer history
we are living through and the folks who came before us.

QUEER PEOPLE THROUGHOUT HISTORY

Queer folks are all over history. We have been a part of
every century, every empire, every civilization, every culture since the dawn of time. As author Sarah Prager points
out in the introduction of her book *Rainbow Revolutionaries:
50 LGBTQ+ People Who Made History,* "LGBTQ+ people have
shaped the world as we know it. From conquerors to com-
posers and artists to activists, the LGBTQ+ community has
made a mark on every century of human existence."

The first queer person I remember learning about in a
history class at school and not on my own was Bayard Rustin. He was a gay Black man, trusted advisor of Dr. Martin
Luther King Jr., and a lead organizer of the 1963 March on
Washington. Rustin is frequently left out of racial justice
curricula because of his queerness; he was arrested in 1953
when he was found having sex with two men, violating the
anti-sodomy laws that existed at the time. The only reason I
learned about Bayard Rustin was because I went to a Quaker
high school and he happened to be Quaker. The fact that he
was queer was merely a footnote. I had of course learned
about people like Eleanor Roosevelt and Virginia Woolf, but
their sexualities, like so many queer people in history, were
made mostly invisible. I learned about the HIV/AIDS crisis
mostly through Jonathan Larson's *Rent* and Tony Kushner's
Angels in America.[30] And so much of the brutal history of queer
suffering features queer people in horrific circumstances like

---

30 If you couldn't already tell, I'm a mostly reformed musical theater
dork.

Brandon Teena's story in *Boys Don't Cry*, and biopics like *Milk* that celebrated Harvey Milk and his accomplishments before depicting his assassination.

I didn't learn about Alan Turing, the queer man, the father of modern computer science, and a vital WWII code-breaker, until I was in college. The UK government's way of thanking him for his scientific contribution to the world was by sentencing him to be forcibly sterilized for the crime of homosexuality. Queer people were specifically targeted by Nazis, but my Hebrew school left that part out. That dark time in queer history is where the queer liberation group, ACT UP, got its infamous pink triangle, turning a symbol of great loss and atrocity into a symbol of resistance. You might be recognizing a theme here of queer reclamation!

Much of queer history, that we typically see and hear, is steeped in violence, sickness, death, and struggle. It's no wonder why we grow up believing our lives will be difficult and unhappy when that's what we're told queer lives have been throughout history. Teaching queer history in this way is an active deterrent to queer identity.

So how do these stories of restriction and death and even torture fit in with our joyful mission? What you need to understand here is that queer joy is not something we come to in spite of grief and suffering. I've said it before and I'll say it again: great joy blooms from the soil of great suffering. We cannot wallow in the despair of our history, but neither can we skate over it and celebrate queer love and forget the suffering it was born of. We cannot fall into a toxic positivity that forgets how much we have lost along our way to liberation. We must understand and embrace the totality of our history in order to *choose* joy and find balance in our depictions and stories of our queer history that in tandem recognize hardship and celebrate all we have accomplished. Our ancestors' lives were not completely engulfed in sadness. Many of these people lived full and joyful lives despite the circumstances of their times. We can choose joy and honor everything our queer ancestors have given us (the joy *and* the sorrow) for we would not be where we are today in our movement without them. They suffered so we could thrive and thrive we will.

Western queer history from the past five hundred years might be a bit daunting to approach with young children; it involves police violence, mass death from the AIDS pandemic and the Holocaust genocide, and a whole lot of hurt and pain and suffering. But not all queer history is fraught! There are a lot of incredible achievements that have been made by queer people over the centuries, and those moments of triumph should not be overshadowed by what has been endured. Queer people, like queer history itself, have a lightness and a darkness. That is the nature of human existence!

Even if it's difficult and you might not know how to approach topics like Stonewall or the HIV/AIDS pandemic head-on, there are plenty of ways to incorporate queer history into your world. We need to recalibrate our understanding of history to include queerness.

HOW TO TALK TO KIDS ABOUT STONEWALL

You don't have to wait until your child hits grade school to introduce queer history in their lives. In fact, that's too late! Young people need to hear stories of the queer people who came before them.

One of the most important stories of queer history you could tell them is about the Stonewall riots. There is quite a bit of violence associated with this story, so in order to avoid scaring children, we can carefully frame this particular story for young people. The story of Stonewall is about so much more than its harm (although that's a very important part of what happened); it's a story of resilience, courage, resistance, and *friendship*.

You can begin with the friendship between Marsha "Pay No Mind" Johnson, a Black trans woman, and Sylvia Rivera, a Latina trans woman. They are generally credited with helping to incite the Stonewall riots, along with Stormé DeLarverie, a gender nonconforming butch Black lesbian, who sometimes worked security at the Stonewall Inn. I always start this story with their friendship, and talk about what kinds of things the kid(s) I'm telling the story to like to do with their friends. Marsha and Sylvia, for example, loved to go out dancing!

And here's where we bring in the ideas of fairness. Marsha and Sylvia were trans women and people, like them, who were a part of the LGBTQ+ community in the 1960s, weren't allowed in certain places simply because of who they were. The Stonewall Inn in the West Village was one of a few places where LGBTQ+ people could go where it was safe for them to be themselves. So on June 28 in 1969, Marsha and Sylvia went dancing at the Stonewall Inn, where Stormé was working, and they danced the night away.

Until there was a loud knock at the door. Take pause here to play up the dramatics of the moment and ask the kids who they think is at the door. They might know the answer: a police officer came in and told Marsha and Sylvia and Stormé that they couldn't dance anymore. They weren't allowed to be there because of who they were: queer and trans women of color, among the LGBTQ+ community, in one of the only places where it was safe(r) for them to be themselves.

Here's where we lean back into the emphasis on friendship and how our doorknob approach comes into play. Communicate the emotional weight of this incredibly important story without getting into details around the violence that might scare a young child. We can ask: When Marsha and Sylvia and Stormé and their friends hear that they can't dance anymore, what would it feel like if someone barged in on your party and told you that you couldn't dance with your friends anymore, because of who you are? Connecting a story like this to a concept that kids can understand is incredibly powerful. Kids can feel the brutal unfairness of the story through this telling. And when you tell them that Marsha and Sylvia and Stormé stood up to the police officers and said, "No more!," they can feel the weight of the moment even more so than they might with all the gory details.

This particular retelling doesn't lie about or edit out the violence, but it reframes this historical moment in a way that kids can relate to the emotional core of the story. How is it unfair that Marsha, Sylvia, and their friends were treated this way (specifically by police), and how can we personally understand the weight of that unfairness for ourselves and how it might affect us in our lives? These ideas are central in galvanizing and inspiring young people toward activism. This story proves that queer histories can still pack an emotional punch even when they are told in a developmentally relevant way. We're not erasing the violence of this story, we're simply refocusing on the people and relationships involved in order for kids to understand the weight of this particular historical moment.

Kids can understand this pivotal night through the eyes of best friends like Marsha and Sylvia. They can understand the importance of the story as the beginning of the LGBTQ+ movement as we know it today. It's a creation myth and an origin story that deserves every retelling.

PRIDE, KIDS, AND KINK DISCOURSE

You might have come to this book thinking I was going to talk a *lot* about Pride. As you can see, there's a *lot* more to bringing up kids in a queer and gender-affirming way than bringing them to a Pride parade. Queer people are queer 365-and-a-quarter days of the year, not only during the thirty days in June. It's true that Pride is important as a time of celebration of our identities and communities, and a tribute to Stonewall and queer history, but it's not everything. On a basic level, you should be sure to talk to your kids about Pride Month and its origins, and celebrate Pride in your household and take your kids to a Pride parade or two. But there's one more thing I want to talk about: *kink*.

There's a discourse that pops up on Twitter like clockwork before and during Pride Month, condemning kink at Pride parades because it's not "family-friendly." Let's pause for a moment and break that down. What do I mean when I say "kink"? In this context, we're mostly talking about queers who march in the parades decked out in leather from harnesses to choke collars to ass-less chaps. But that's one small sliver of what kink is. "Kink" is a much larger concept that describes nonconventional sexual practices, concepts, or fantasies. The kink we are talking about in this example is leather kink or leather culture, where someone likes to use leather garments like jackets, vests, boots, chaps, and harnesses for sexual purposes.

So how do you approach this in a way kids can understand it? Kids simply don't associate leather with kink or sex
or kinky sex for that matter. They see leather as leather, a
clothing material and just that. When a kid sees someone
decked out in leather at a Pride parade, they probably think
they're wearing a cool outfit, or that they might be hot wearing leather on a warm summer day. The sex connotations of
leather almost surely won't occur to kids since it is very unlikely that they are actually watching someone have kinky
leather sex at a Pride parade, because it is outside and in
public. When your child asks, "Why are they wearing that?"
they are asking about that person's clothes, not about the
kind of sex they like to have while they wear it. It's in the
same vein as the answer to "Where do babies come from?"
We have to listen to and answer the *actual* question kids ask,
not the question us grown-ups *think* they are asking.

What you can focus on here is what about kink and
leather is age-relevant to the child. It's the leather clothes
themselves! You don't have to get into the sex part if you
don't want to; the truth of it is that kink is an adult way of
playing dress-up and pretend! And that's all you need to say
to answer that child: "Some adults like to dress up and play
pretend." Kink and kids can coexist at Pride with the right
explanation. And if you want to take this particular opportunity to scaffold a conversation around consent and pleasure,
by all means go ahead!

THE HIV/AIDS CRISIS

At some point in your queer history lessons with the young
folks in your lives, you'll have to cover the HIV/AIDS crisis. Because of the COVID-19 pandemic, you're probably an

expert at talking about sickness and disease and pandemics with your child.

The HIV/AIDS crisis was an incredibly important part of recent LGBTQ+ history and still is an ongoing pandemic. Because of that fact, it might even help you to talk to young folks about COVID-19 and provide historical context to what is happening and immediately felt in their lives. Stories help young people process what is happening around them, and the story of the HIV/AIDS crisis might feel almost comforting in its familiarity. Talking about it also helps destigmatize HIV/AIDS status. Even Sesame Workshop has an HIV+ muppet in their South African programs because the disease is so prevalent there, particularly in children whose mothers are HIV+.

In order to talk about the HIV/AIDS crisis, you don't need to talk about gay sex. Yes, it can spread through anal sex, but there are also other ways that HIV/AIDS can spread: blood transfusion (although that is incredibly rare now), needles, and in utero. However, that's not particularly important to this conversation; what *is* important is talking about who is and was affected most by the HIV/AIDS pandemic. That's the LGBTQ+ community, specifically gay men—Black gay men and trans women are currently the most at risk. And we talk about how a lot of people in America, particularly in the 1980s and 1990s, ignored the HIV/AIDS pandemic.

AIDS was originally called gay-related immune deficiency, or GRID. Even though public health officials first knew about the disease in July 1981, fear of the "gay plague" spread as quickly as the plague itself. Queer men dealt with the dual fears of their own mortality and potentially being outed through their illness. Even as the cases and death toll grew, news outlets were hesitant to cover it. *The New York Times* initially reported on HIV/AIDS in July 1981, but didn't give the pandemic front-page coverage until May 25, 1983, two years and thousands of deaths later. Imagine watching a mysterious illness pick off your friends one by one, spreading through whole communities of people and not seeing a single headline about it in the news.

At the time, HIV/AIDS was little more than a punch line in President Reagan's White House press briefings. The federal government under Reagan was silent, and his administration's acute neglect was obvious in the lack of urgency to research the virus. Two years into the HIV/AIDS crisis there was little to no federal funding dedicated to the pandemic. Compare that to the almost immediate governmental response to COVID-19. The differences in urgency responding to these two ongoing pandemics are stark.

In her piece "'Where Was This When My Friends Were Dying?': HIV Crisis Survivors Reflect on Coronavirus" for Them.us, Sarah Prager points out that, compared to the COVID-19 pandemic, "the HIV/AIDS crisis saw our government sentence an entire queer generation to death by ignoring calls for treatment development." The pharmaceutical company Moderna announced in August 2021 that they are *finally* starting human trials for an HIV vaccine. That's a full *forty years* and *36.3 million deaths* after the World Health Organization recognized HIV/AIDS as a pandemic in 1981.

We remember those we've lost through the AIDS Memorial Quilt, which was originally conceived in 1985 by San Francisco gay rights activist Cleve Jones. The Quilt was first displayed at the National Mall in Washington, DC, on October 11, 1987, during the Second National March on Washington for Lesbian and Gay Rights. That original version of the Quilt included 1,920 panels, each individually handmade in memory of a loved one who died of AIDS. Now, the AIDS Memorial Quilt weighs in at fifty-four tons and includes over fifty thousand panels. According to the National AIDS Memorial—today's keepers of the Quilt—where it has been returned to its original home in San Francisco, the Quilt remains "the premiere symbol of the AIDS pandemic, a living memorial to a generation lost to AIDS and an important HIV prevention education tool . . . the Quilt is considered the largest community arts project in history."

While Stonewall provides an origin story for the LGBTQ+ rights movement, the cornerstones of the modern movement started with the HIV/AIDS crisis. The marriage equality movement as we know it today first started because when loved ones died of AIDS, their partners and chosen family weren't able to visit them in the hospital, or claim their belongings after they died because they were not married. Our families and our rights to be married as queer couples exist because of Marsha, because of Sylvia, and because of the thousands of queer elders who died of HIV/AIDS, and we continue to fight and progress forward in their names and in the name of queer liberation for generations to come. That's why it was so important to my wife and I that we had a queer mentor of hers give a speech to emphasize the historical importance of our legal union and connection to the larger queer movement during our wedding ceremony.

Something I personally think about a lot is the loss of a generation of queer elders. What would queer liberation look like today if almost an entire generation of queer people hadn't been wiped out? Would we have more queer people in senior professional positions with more wealth, power, experience, and knowledge to distribute? Maybe I'm giving too much benefit of the doubt, but I wonder if it would have been easier for me to find mentorship earlier in my career if so many queer lives hadn't been lost from the generations that came before mine. If I wouldn't have had to be a "trail-blazer" in my own right because someone would have come before me and could have passed the torch. But that's all wishful thinking. I'll never know the answer to that conditional. Let's forge onward and honor those who came before us by taking up the torch that fell and passing it along while we can.

HOW TO EXPLAIN THE HIV/AIDS CRISIS TO KIDS

As you talk to your kid about the HIV/AIDS crisis, you can use any words and ideas you've already talked about related to the COVID-19 pandemic. You should purposefully avoid classifying HIV/AIDS as a "gay disease" because it's (1) not true and (2) a common (and harmful) misconception. Let's shift the framing to give an accurate explanation.

AIDS is an illness that attacks someone's immune system, which is what keeps us from getting sick all the time. When most bodies encounter a disease or sickness, their immune system kicks into gear to protect them and fight it off. But someone with AIDS doesn't have an immune system that works properly, leaving their bodies defenseless to different kinds of illnesses and infections. AIDS is caused by a virus called HIV. HIV is transmitted through blood and other bodily fluids, but it can't be passed through the air like COVID-19. Some things that can pass the HIV infection from one person to another are unsterilized needles, blood transfusions (again, this is very rare now!), and sex. Sex is just one way that HIV can transfer, but it's not the only way! Lots of different people can get HIV, but it especially affects gay men, transgender women, and Black and Brown LGBTQ+ people. There currently isn't a cure for AIDS, but there are preventative medications people can take so they cannot transmit their own HIV infection or get it from someone else.

LGBTQ+ HISTORY IN PROGRESS

One of the most exciting parts about LGBTQ+ history is that we are currently living in it. It's hard to live through pivotal moments in history, but it can also be exciting! We can be witness to and even contribute to the advancement of LGBTQ+ rights within our short lifetimes. The things that are happening now—like the fights for marriage equality and against workplace discrimination, the Equality Act and the pushback on anti-trans legislation—that's all modern American LGBTQ+ history. And that's not counting the LGBTQ+ history that's being made around the world, as more countries legalize same-sex marriage, and the fight for equality continues in places like Russia and Hungary, where there are strict anti-LGBTQ+ propaganda laws and their queer communities mostly exist underground. One day soon, these events that we are currently living through will be taught in history books as important points along the road to equality for the LGBTQ+ community.

Talk about what's currently happening with LGBTQ+ rights with your kids, and keep informed yourself! There's a *lot* going on in the world. It's important to talk about and understand the current state of things and stay informed, especially beyond major news outlets that don't always cover LGBTQ+ issues adequately. Celebrate what folks like Chase Strangio, Raquel Willis, Laverne Cox, Janet Mock, Nick Adams, Elliot Page, Tourmaline, and ALOK—only a few of today's movement leaders—are accomplishing right now. Make sure you're participating in your local LGBTQ+ Pride parade and family-friendly Pride activities in June every year! And support small queer and trans–owned businesses instead of funding corporate rainbow capitalism.

REFLECTION
That was a lot to cover! We went from expanding our vocabulary and explaining more advanced topics around gender and sexuality to your kindergarteners, to breaking down the ways different identities and social issues affect queer communities, to building your family's activist practice and supplementing your kid's education with important LGBTQ+ history. Now you can more easily talk to kids about the kinds of people who make up the LGBTQ+ community as a whole. You can have conversations with your kids about different parts of our identities, so you can begin to fold queer histories into your lives.

We've done a lot of the heavy lifting and continued to transform your at-home and classroom libraries; we've established new practices and are more conscious of our privileges and marginalizations. Now it's time to finally shift fully from the page to the great wide world. Maybe you've soaked up all of this information and started to do this work, but between you and the kids in your life, it doesn't quite feel like enough yet. Maybe it feels like you are waking up to all of these oppressive systems and you want to *do* something about it, but you feel overwhelmed and unsure of how to dive in and start doing the work that's much bigger than you or me, or even your immediate family unit or your classroom. That's where it gets *exciting*! This is where you can start to feel like you are a part of something bigger than yourself. This is where you and the young folks in your life can become *change-makers* and spread queer joy. We've got this!

KEY TAKEAWAYS

- Kindergarten+ is when you can start getting a *lot* more specific and dig deep into concepts where you already have an established shared understanding.

- Make sure you include queer, trans, and nonbinary perspectives and voices when you approach topics like race, class, religion, mental health, and disability.

- Think critically and *creatively* about how you can actively bring justice principles into your day-to-day lives with your kid.

- Work on stepping up your allyship toward the principles of comradery.

- There's no one way to be an activist!

- Pay attention to LGBTQ+ history in progress as you fill in your knowledge gaps on the queer history of the past.

CONCLUSION

You made it! You've reached this point and done all this work and learned to *spread queer joy*. As you've read, you've understood why we are doing this work: the mental health and safety of LGBTQ+ youth, abuse prevention, allyship and comradery with marginalized groups, and the well-being of the kids in your life. But as you go into the world, I want you to remember the *big* why.

The big why is about the future. The big why is the world that ought to be, the future of our species and life on Earth. The big why is true progress. We are detangling our own prejudices and biases that we have inherited, rewriting our journeys and our stories beyond what we have been told we are capable of, and we are actively disrupting the systemic patterns being passed on to our youth. We can work to change things in the present moment, but none of that matters if the next generation upholds these systems. We have to *break* these patterns.

As we work to dismantle our oppressive systems, we must give today's young people the tools and tactics they will need in order to rebuild it for themselves when we pass the generational baton. The work we are doing here together is the labor of dismantling, and it is *also* a strategy for rebuilding. Because in order to rebuild, we must first draw blueprints. This work is what allows for the creative capacity to imagine a better and kinder world for humanity. You are a queer futurist and we are building a whole new world together.

There are so many different kinds of imaginings of this utopic future: trans and nonbinary people looking for a new understanding of gender beyond the binary; Black and Brown people calling for reparations, abolition of police and prisons, and the respect they deserve; Indigenous peoples calling for their land back and stewardship of our sick planet; disabled communities calling for spaces that accommodate, account for, and go beyond consideration of their needs; and so much more. This better world is a vast landscape and no one community, let alone one person, can even begin to imagine the Platonic ideal of this utopia. But we can do what is within our powers and our privileges to *try*.

On this grandiose scale, it is unlikely that we will see the true fruits of our labor play out within our lifetime. But that's not to say this work is thankless. A few weeks ago, I got a DM on the *Queer Kid Stuff* Instagram page from a long-time fan of the show. They said they watch our Pride videos with their family every June for Pride Month like they watch the Grinch movie on Christmas. One of their children came out as trans recently, and their sibling wrote a picture book about having a trans sibling.

I get stories like these in my inbox *all the time*. From two-mom families who felt validated and represented in something they could show their kids, from progressive straight parents who were looking for a way to introduce nonbinary pronouns to their kids, and from kids themselves, and even high school students, who "wish they had this when they were younger," these are young lives that this work has impacted and changed for the better. I can speechify the large-scale benefits of this work all day long, talking about the future and the benefits to society and convincing you to believe in this work through statistics and personal anecdotes, but the truth of it is that the impact of what we're doing here is about every individual child this work touches. The young people who are still here and need this work. The child who embarks upon their own gender journey instead of falling into the depths of depression, unable to enjoy the gift of youth. The child who doesn't think it's weird that a boy in their class wears dresses to school.

A professor of mine once gave me a note on my senior undergrad thesis to change the wording of a sentence to say that this work "touches lives" instead of "changes lives." That professor was wrong. This work, if we can all do it together, will fundamentally change people's lives, no ifs, ands, or buts. And by changing lives, I believe in the depths of my soul that we can change the world, one kid at a time. There's a long way ahead of us, but the horizon is there and it's waiting for us.

Now, go out and *spread queer joy.*

ADDITIONAL RESOURCES AND BOOK RECOMMENDATIONS

A quick note that these lists are by no means exhaustive. There are so many *incredible* queer and trans books by queer and trans authors that I couldn't possibly include them all here. This list will get you started, but I encourage you to tumble down the rabbit hole and find what best suits you and your kiddos!

FOR YOUR BOARD BOOK READER

First Conversations series by Megan Madison and Jessica Ralli

Yes! No!: A First Conversation About Consent illustrated by Isabel Roxas

Being You: A First Conversation About Gender illustrated by Anne/Andy Passchier

Our Skin: A First Conversation About Race illustrated by Isabel Roxas

A Is for Activist by Innosanto Nagara

The GayBCs by M. L. Webb

Homemade Love by bell hooks,[31] illustrated by Shane W. Evans

Our Rainbow by Little Bee Books

Love Makes a Family by Sophie Beer

Pride 1 2 3 by Michael Joosten, illustrated by Wednesday Holmes

FOR YOUR PICTURE BOOK READER

Classics written by queer authors:

Goodnight Moon by Margaret Wise Brown, illustrated by Clement Hurd

The Runaway Bunny by Margaret Wise Brown, illustrated by Clement Hurd

Frog and Toad Are Friends by Arnold Lobel

Strega Nona by Tomie dePaola

George and Martha by James Marshall

Where the Wild Things Are by Maurice Sendak

The Happy Prince and Other Tales by Oscar Wilde

Modern picture books written by queer and trans authors:

Max and Friends series *by Kyle Lukoff, illustrated by Luciano Lozano*

Call Me Max

Max on the Farm

Max and the Talent Show

When Aidan Became a Brother by Kyle Lukoff, illustrated by Kaylani Juanita

---

31 Yes, THE bell hooks wrote board books!

My Rainbow by Trinity and DeShanna Neal, illustrated by Art Twink

Sylvia and Marsha Start a Revolution! by Joy Michael Ellison, illustrated by Teshika Silver

The Boy & the Bindi by Vivek Shraya, illustrated by Rajni Perera

From the Stars in the Sky to the Fish in the Sea by Kai Cheng Thom, illustrated by Wai-Yant Li and Kai Yun Ching

What Makes a Baby by Cory Silverberg, illustrated by Fiona Smyth

What's an Abortion, Anyway? by Carly Manes, illustrated by Emulsify

Kind Like Marsha: Learning from LGBTQ+ Leaders by Sarah Prager, illustrated by Cheryl "Ras" Thuesday

Phoenix Goes to School by Michelle and Phoenix Finch, illustrated by Sharon Davey

I Am Jazz by Jessica Herthel and Jazz Jennings, pictures by Shelagh McNicholas

The Hips on the Drag Queen Go Swish, Swish, Swish by Lil Miss Hot Mess, illustrated by Olga de Dios Ruiz

They Call Me Mix/Me Llaman Maestre by Lourdes Rivas, illustrated by Breena Nuñez

Umi & Uma: The Story of Two Mommies and a Baby by Nyesha and Samantha Davis-Williams

The Nonbinary Bunny by Maia Kobabe

My Maddy by Gayle E. Pitman, illustrated by Violet Tobacco

This Day in June by Gayle E. Pitman, illustrated by Kristyna Litten

Peanut Goes for the Gold by Jonathan Van Ness, illustrated by Gillian Reid

Stacey's Not a Girl by Colt Keo-Meier, illustrated by Jesse Yang

And Tango Makes Three by Justin Richardson and Peter Parnell, illustrated by Henry Cole

Kapaemahu by Hinaleimoana Wong-Kalu, Dean Hamer, and Joe Wilson, illustrated by Daniel Sousa

Call Me Tree/Llámame árbol by Maya Christina Gonzalez

Payden's Pronoun Party by Blue Jaryn, illustrated by Xochitl Cornejo

Hooray, What a Day!/¡Viva, Qué Día! by Sunny Allis

Every Body Is a Rainbow: A Kid's Guide to Bodies Across the Gender Spectrum by Caroline Carter, PsyD, illustrated by Mathias Ball

Picture Books from Flamingo Rampant

Flamingo Rampant is a trans and queer–owned and operated indie picture book publisher founded by S. Bear Bergman. FR produces "feminist, racially-diverse, LGBTQ-positive children's books, in an effort to bring visibility and positivity to the reading landscape of children everywhere. [They] make books kids love that love them right back, bedtime stories for beautiful dreams, and books that make kids of all kinds say with pride: that kid's just like me!" I recommend *all* of their books, but here are a few of my personal favorites:

47,000 Beads written by Koja Adeyoha and Angel Adeyoha, illustrated by Holly McGillis

M Is for Mustache: A Pride ABC Book by Catherine Hernandez, illustrated by Marisa Firebaugh

Rachel's Christmas Boat by Sophie Labelle

The Last Place You Look by j wallace skelton, illustrated by Justin Alves

The Zero Dads Club by Angel Adeyoha, illustrated by
    Aubrey Williams
A Princess of Great Daring! by Tobi Hill-Meyer, illustrated
    by Elenore Toczynski

Picture Books from Reflection Press
Reflection Press is another queer–owned and operated indie
publisher founded by partners Maya Gonzalez and Mathew
SG. Reflection Press "produce[s] materials that support a
strong sense of individuality along with a community model
of real inclusion. [Their] materials teach social awareness,
critical thinking skills, as well as provide much needed reflection and respect." Here are a few of their titles that I love:

They She He Me: Free to Be! by Maya Christina Gonzalez
    and Matthew SG
*When We Love Someone We Sing to Them/Cuando Amamos
    Cantamos* by Ernesto Javier Martínez, illustrated by
    Maya Gonzalez
*The Gender Wheel: A Story about Bodies and Gender for Every
    Body* by Maya Gonzalez

FOR YOUR CHAPTER BOOK READER
Different Kinds of Fruit by Kyle Lukoff
Too Bright to See by Kyle Lukoff
I Kissed Shara Wheeler by Casey McQuiston
The Fabulous Zed Watson! by Basil Sylvester and Kevin
    Sylvester
Melissa by Alex Gino
Hurricane Child by Kacen Callender
Zenobia July by Lisa Bunker
The Best at It by Maulik Pancholy

Meow or Never by Jazz Taylor

The Insiders by Mark Oshiro

Ana on the Edge by A. J. Sass

This Is Our Rainbow: 16 Stories of Her, Him, Them, and Us, an all-queer anthology, edited by Katherine Locke and Nicole Melleby

FOR YOUR GRAPHIC NOVEL AND COMICS READER

Rainbow Revolutionaries: 50 LGBTQ+ People Who Made History by Sarah Prager, illustrated by Sarah Papworth

Sex Is a Funny Word: A Book about Bodies, Feelings, and YOU by Cory Silverberg and Fiona Smyth

Nimona by ND Stevenson

The Girl from the Sea by Molly Knox Ostertag

The Lumberjanes series, created by ND Stevenson, Grace Ellis, Shannon Watters, and Gus Allen

The Witch Boy series by Molly Knox Ostertag

The Witch Boy

The Hidden Witch

The Midwinter Witch

The Tea Dragon Trilogy by K. O'Neill

The Tea Dragon Society

The Tea Dragon Festival

The Tea Dragon Tapestry

Mooncakes by Suzanne Walker, illustrated by Wendy Xu

The Prince and the Dressmaker by Jen Wang

The Magic Fish by Trung Le Nguyen

FOR FAMILY TV TIME:[32]
Preschool

Pinecone & Pony, developed by Stephanie Kaliner, based
    on the book *The Princess and the Pony* by Kate Beaton
The Fabulous Show with Fay and Fluffy, from Lopii Productions
Video: "The Blue's Clues Pride Parade Sing-Along, ft.
    Nina West!"
Ridley Jones, created by Chris Nee (creator of *Doc McStuffins*
    and *Vampirina*)
The Bravest Knight Who Ever Lived, from Big Bad Boo Studios
Queer Kid Stuff
Short Film: "The Healer Stones of Kapaemahu"

Kids & Family Animation

Steven Universe, created by Rebecca Sugar
Danger & Eggs, created by Shadi Petosky and Mike Owens
Dead End: Paranormal Park, created by Hamish Steele
She-Ra and the Princesses of Power, created by ND Stevenson
The Owl House, created by Dana Terrace
Craig of the Creek, created by Matt Burnett, Ben Levin,
    and Shauna McGarry
Gravity Falls, created by Alex Hirsch
The Loud House, created by Chris Savino, Michael Rubiner

BOOKS FOR YOU

Raising Antiracist Children: A Practical Parenting Guide by
    Britt Hawthorne with Natasha Yglesias
*Social Justice Parenting: How to Raise Compassionate, Anti-
    Racist, Justice-Minded Kids in an Unjust World* by Dr.
    Traci Baxley

---

32 Note that I don't have any feature film recommendations on here . . .

Raising Them: Our Adventure in Gender Creative Parenting
    by Kyl Myers
The Natural Mother of the Child: A Memoir of Nonbinary Parent-hood by Krys Malcolm Belc
Histories of the Transgender Child by Jules Gill-Peterson
Unconditional: A Guide to Loving and Supporting Your LGBTQ Child by Telaina Eriksen
Gender Queer: A Memoir by Maia Kobabe
Sissy: A Coming-of-Gender Story by Jacob Tobia
Seeing Gender: An Illustrated Guide to Identity and Expression by Iris Gottlieb
Trust Kids! Stories on Youth Autonomy and Confronting Adult Supremacy, edited by carla joy bergman

DOCUMENTARIES FOR YOU

Disclosure, a film by Sam Feder and Amy Scholder, available on Netflix
Changing the Game, directed by Michael Barnett, available on Hulu
Framing Agnes, directed by Chase Joynt and Kristen Schilt
I Love You, You Hate Me, documentary series directed by Tommy Avallone, available on Peacock
Won't You Be My Neighbor?, directed by Morgan Neville, available on Netflix

PODCASTS FOR YOU

Rainbow Parenting, created and hosted by yours truly
Gender Reveal, hosted by Tuck Woodstock
If These Ovaries Could Talk, hosted by queer parents Jaimie Kelton and E Bradshaw
Rad Child Podcast, hosted by Seth Day

Outspoken Voices: A Podcast of LGBTQ+ Families presented by Family Equality

A FEW SMALL QUEER AND TRANS-CREATED AND OWNED PROJECTS AND ORGANIZATIONS

The Gender Wheel

- Another project from Maya Gonzalez! It's a "tool and a concept first developed . . . to express the dynamic and infinite nature of gender." It is another framework and educational curriculum to talk about and teach ideas around gender to children!

Woke Kindergarten

- Created by Ki Gross, Woke Kindergarten is a "global, abolitionist early childhood ecosystem & visionary creative portal supporting children, families, educators, and organizers in their commitment to abolitionist early education and pro-Black and queer and trans liberation."

Galaxy Community Circle

- Created by Eli Dinh, Galaxy Community Circle is a "space to celebrate and affirm gender diverse children ages 4–12." This is a digital community space for queer, trans, and nonbinary kids!

The Genderbread Person

- Now in its fourth iteration, The Genderbread Person is a popular educational tool created by Sam Killermann that helps break down the different facets of gender.

Pop'n'Olly

- This YouTube channel started by actor Olly Pike has turned into a thriving business based in the UK creating books and "LGBT+ education for children, parents, carers & teachers."

Gender Inclusive Classrooms
- A website created by teachers for teachers! Two queer and trans teachers (Kieran and Katy) create gender-inclusive content "dedicated to equipping educators with the tools they need to foster safe, welcoming gender-inclusive classrooms."

LARGE ORGANIZATIONS YOU PROBABLY ALREADY KNOW ABOUT

PFLAG

GLSEN Gay, Lesbian & Straight Education Network

GLAAD The Gay and Lesbian Alliance Against Defamation

Family Equality

The Trevor Project

Trans Lifeline

ACKNOWLEDGMENTS

Wowie there are so many people to thank! The cliché that "it takes a village" is a cliché for a reason!

To my inimitable agent, Claire Draper. You were one of the very first people willing to take a chance on me and this wild mission of mine. I am endlessly grateful for your collaboration and your steadfastness through the many years it's taken us to push this book from proposal to submission to revision to SOLD! You've been my champion and cheerleader for years and I'm so glad you were the first on my team. I owe you a pickleback!

To Sylvan Creekmore, the editor who read my mess of a proposal and saw what could one day be a much better book. You were my first big yes and I will always remember that. And to Hannah Phillips who hopped in fearlessly mid-drafting with this first-time author. Thank you for bringing a much needed shift in perspective and for carrying this thing to the finish line.

To everyone from the cover designer to the sensitivity reader to the copy editor and all the other folks who have touched this book on its way to publication. Thank you so much for making this book worthy of a spot on readers' bookshelves and for catching the typos and extra commas that would make my high school English teacher cringe! And a heartfelt thank-you to my readers and blurbers who took the time to read early versions of this book. I sent it to you because I hold an incredible amount of adoration for you and am honored that you took the time out of your busy day to read my words.

To everyone I interviewed and whose wisdom I used in this book! Justine Ang Fonte, Kyle Lukoff, Sarah Prager, Dr. Jason Rafferty, Trystan Reece, Megan Madison, Philip Dawkins, Jules Gill-Peterson, and Dr. Kyl Myers! Thank you for your work, I'm beyond honored to be in your company.

Thank you to my QKS team! To the original troupe: Elliot, Montana, Emmie, Hannah, and Meghan. You've been with me since the beginning, and none of my work or career would be a reality without your collaboration. And to my small but mighty team, past and present! Collin, Val, Genny, L, Elise, Kit, Andrew, and Natasha and the Take-3Talent team! Thank you for hoping on board and taking this weird and wild journey alongside me! And to the folks over at Multitude Productions—Amanda, Eric, Brandon, and Mischa—who helped me turn a book into a podcast and gave this work a life beyond the page.

To my community and my cheerleaders! You've seen the ups and the downs of my career so far and through this particular leg of the journey. You've cheered me on days when I wanted to throw my laptop out the window and when I got to announce this project to the world.

To the parents whose names I wrote on a sticky note in my office to help remind me who I was writing to: Hannah and Will, Jaya and John, Jessie and Dan, and Audrey and

Hunter! You helped me remember who I was talking to and it forced me into new and necessary perspectives. Thank you for being my model audience!

To all my parents and siblings: Mom, Dad, Ned, Katie, Rose, Grace, and Perri. Thank you for sitting through my book updates over the last two years and asking how it was going even when I was on the struggle bus! Thank you to my dear Wednesday and my cousin Amanda in particular who've been boons throughout this process.

And finally to my incredible wife, Hilary. I am the luckiest wusband in the whole wide world. I got to announce this book the week of our wedding, and I don't think I'll ever be able to top the high of that week. Thank you for bearing with me on my dark cloud days, and for popping the champagne with me at every chance we get to celebrate. I love you most.

And of course, to Georgie, the furry love of my life. You can't read this, but thank you for the snuggles and kisses.

INDEX

ABOUT THE AUTHOR

Ella Pennington

Lindz Amer (they/them) makes queer stuff for kids and families. They started on this wild and winding career path when they created *Queer Kid Stuff*—an award-winning original LGBTQ+ educational web series for all ages—which has reached millions of families. They perform at libraries, schools, and theaters all over the world, spreading queer joy and work on numerous projects that bring queer and trans representation into mainstream children's media. In 2019, they gave a viral TED Talk on the importance of talking to kids about gender and sexuality. They currently write for preschool television and also host the parenting podcast *Rainbow Parenting,* as well as *Activist, You!* for kids, featuring interviews with youth activists. Their work has been featured by *Good Morning America*, Kidscreen, *Teen Vogue*, and *Parents* magazine. They live in New England with their wife and spunky cattle dog mix named Georgie.